The Survival Guide
for Gen X Leaders

The Survival Guide for Gen X Leaders

Building the Bridge from the Great Resignation to the Multigenerational Future We All Want

Amy Morrison

ROWMAN & LITTLEFIELD
Lanham • Boulder • New York • London

Published by Rowman & Littlefield
An imprint of The Rowman & Littlefield Publishing Group, Inc.
4501 Forbes Boulevard, Suite 200, Lanham, Maryland 20706
www.rowman.com

86-90 Paul Street, London EC2A 4NE, United Kingdom

British Library Cataloguing in Publication Information Available

Library of Congress Cataloging-in-Publication Data

Names: Morrison, Amy, 1972– author.
Title: The survival guide for Gen X leaders : building the bridge from the great resignation to the multigenerational future we all want / Amy Morrison.
Description: Lanham : Rowman & Littlefield, [2024] | Includes bibliographical references and index. | Summary: "The Survival Guide for Gen X Leaders provides hope and pragmatic tips to guide organizations and institutes through times of tremendous transition"— Provided by publisher.
Identifiers: LCCN 2024005896 (print) | LCCN 2024005897 (ebook) | ISBN 9781475870978 (cloth) | ISBN 9781475870985 (paperback) | ISBN 9781475870992 (epub)
Subjects: LCSH: Leadership. | Generation X. | Intergenerational relations. | Organizational effectiveness.
Classification: LCC HD57.7 .M6745 2024 (print) | LCC HD57.7 (ebook) | DDC 658.4/092—dc23/eng/20240215
LC record available at https://lccn.loc.gov/2024005896
LC ebook record available at https://lccn.loc.gov/2024005897

Contents

Introduction

THE PANDEMIC, THE GREAT RESIGNATION, AND PREPARING FOR THE FUTURE

It is July 2022, and I have just returned from a summer retreat for Washington State's Community and Technical College presidents. From the outside, it looked like any other gathering of leaders—a lot of coffee, pretty good meals, a windowless conference room with beige curtains to keep us focused on the PowerPoint at the front of the room, a semi-remote location to keep us talking to each other, thoughtful and learned presentations, committee work, and yes, a lot of hallway conversations.

However, this retreat was very different from the retreats I previously attended. This summer gathering marked the beginning of my tenth year as college president, and it was our first retreat where we began the transition out of the COVID-19 pandemic emergency phase. And, most distinctly, it was the first meeting where we all truly felt the breathtaking impacts of our own localized version of the Great Resignation, as multiple presidents and chancellors with *over 100 years* of collective executive leadership retired.

To make matters more challenging, these key leaders had left and/or were planning to leave our community and technical college system within a six-month period from June to December 2022, with more retirements and transitions anticipated in 2023 and beyond. The exiting of our long-term colleagues, their experience, historical knowledge, and the awareness of pending retirements were palpable and sometimes unsettling.

I suspect if you are reading this book, you too are at midlife, serving in a leadership role, and looking around wondering how you went from always being the youngest in the room (with your Boomer colleagues) to being the senior leader. Whether you are in higher education, education, non-profit, or business, generational shifts are playing out across the United States, exacerbated and fast-tracked by the pandemic.

As a Gen Xer surrounded primarily by Boomer colleagues during my entire career, I knew in my mid-twenties that at some point they would retire and I would be left with other Gen Xers and some Millennials (although at the beginning of my career, I really didn't work with many Millennials, just Boomers, a couple of Xers, and some remaining Traditionalists). While I knew this day was coming, I could have never predicted that most Boomer retirements would come within six months on the heels of a once-in-a-century global pandemic.

This book is for Gen X leaders (born between 1965 and 1980, and yes, you already know who you are) at all levels who are suddenly looking around and realizing that the Boomers are heading out to a big party called retirement, and you are left with the broom in hand leading the Millennial and Gen Z clean-up crews.

Chances are you are not retiring anytime soon, even if you'd like to. I suspect you will continue to lead for years to come, given the current leadership vacuum left by the Great Resignation. Given the fact that we are still many years out from our own retirements and that we have all been told that social security may be insolvent just about the time we are set to retire as a generation in 2036, the bottom line is, we're going to be at this for a while.

Let's talk for a moment about that clean-up crew that you are now leading (some Boomers, fellow Gen Xers, Millennials, and Gen Zers). We all know our colleagues are *very tired* after a couple of long years of the COVID-19 pandemic. Who can blame them, with things like unspeakable grief and loss, a Racial Reckoning that we have not seen since the Civil Rights movement, a backlash to that reckoning, mass shootings, political division, a political insurrection, inflation, war in Europe, war in the Middle East, an unprecedented youth mental health crisis, long COVID, labor shortages, to name a few challenges.

We Are Now the Adults in the Room

Let's call a spade a spade; this is a very tough time to be the adult in the room, leading our teams, organizations, and communities within a sudden vacuum of Boomer leadership. I also want to add that many of us find ourselves smack in the middle of life. For many of us, this means that we are raising Gen Z children as well as caring for ailing parents whose health has been dramatically impacted by the isolation of the pandemic. This book is my humble way of saying I see you, hear you, and stand with you—with a lot of humility and in service to our families, communities, and organizations we care about deeply.

As difficult as this time is right now for many of us individually and our generation collectively, I would assert that this is the perfect time for our generation to step forward and build a bridge to the future, a future that we want to create with Boomers, Millennials, and Gen Zers. And why, do you ask, is now *our* time?

As Gen Xers, we were raised in an equally uncertain time without many answers. We are used to being left to our own devices (and, thankfully, with a primarily device-free childhood). We are the original latchkey kids who came home after school, opened up a bag of BBQ potato chips (we didn't worry then about what chemicals might be in those potato chips), hung out with our siblings, and listened to Oprah's wisdom before our parents—some divorced—came home from work. A note of personal privilege: Oprah, if by chance you ever read this, I, too, am among the millions of Gen X latchkey kids whom you helped to raise. Thank you; I am forever grateful.

This is our time as we are fiercely independent, we know how to work with others, are pragmatic, and can remain calm under pressure. We may be best known for our music and flannel shirts (yes, I grew up in Seattle in the 1990s and still love Pearl Jam and, as a Bremerton native, Sir Mix-a-Lot). And we may be remembered as the only generation that does not have our own presi-dent—*yet* (I'm engaging my growth mindset on this one). And here we are still, the undercounted, underappreciated generation that has been sneered at for years or, even more likely, ignored altogether. Like it or not, this is our moment to step into the arena (thank you, President Theodore Roosevelt and Brené Brown), clean up this mess, and build a bridge to the future we all want to see, even if we don't get a lot of credit for our work.

Let me take a moment to tell you what this book is *not* about. This book is not meant to bash Boomers (who can blame them for retiring *en masse* after the last couple of years?) or Millennials and Gen Z—we are *all* in this together. And to make sure you know how committed I am to not genera-tion bashing, my husband is a Boomer, his son is a Millennial, I am a Gen Xer, and my son is Gen Z. So there you go, four generations in one loving, blended family.

This book is really meant to validate that you are not alone with your broom in hand, trying to figure out how to clean up this post-pandemic, post-Great Resignation mess and build a bridge to a more stable future for all of us. And I would like to do so in a typical Gen X pragmatic, approachable way. At the end of every section of this book, I'll ask you some questions about your own leadership experience through this unprecedented transition. I'll also summarize key takeaways you can apply today to help you lead, support your health and well-being, and inspire you to keep moving forward.

Shining a Spotlight on Gen X Leadership

I am forever grateful to my friends and colleagues across the country who agreed to be interviewed and share their stories of courage, perseverance, growth, and humility. In their stories, you will see for yourself what Gen X leadership looks like. I hope you will see glimpses of your own story in theirs.

I know that this book may find you at different levels of leadership. You may be a subject matter expert, a mid-level manager, a community leader, an entrepreneur, and yes, even a director, vice-president, or president of your organization. Wherever you may be in your professional or personal world, if you are reading this book, consider yourself a leader. One who is worthy of support right now.

My primary goal with this book is to shine a spotlight on just a few of the amazing Gen X leaders I have had the privilege of working with. I relay, with their approval, of course, their accomplishments during very difficult times, the toll it took, and how they are persevering after leading their organizations and communities through the pandemic. The leaders I spoke to in this book are a small sample of how our generation is contributing and moving us forward in a roll-up-our-sleeves and get-it-done way, without fanfare, without the generational attention, and yet with impact.

This book is written in three parts. First, I discuss why this is a critical moment for Gen X leadership. Second, I review what Gen X leadership looks like through the eyes of exceptional leaders who are leading their organizations and communities and are building bridges to a sustainable and brighter future. The third and final part of this book will include six pragmatic steps to keep you moving forward in your critical work while helping inspire you with your well-being as a leader at the forefront.

Throughout this book, I share my own personal and professional experiences as a Gen Xer and a leader. I do so from my worldview and lived experience, as I define it, as a midlife, white American woman who grew up working-class, first-generation college graduate, served in leadership roles from my mid-twenties to my current day while raising a family and living in Seattle, Washington. My lived experience is my own.

If you connect with my experience and the stories of others throughout this book, that's even better. If your personal and professional experiences are different from ours in this book, I sincerely hope you can find some inspiration and takeaways in this book that will fuel your own leadership journey. The leaders highlighted are not a statistically significant sampling of generational representatives. They are, however, exceptional leaders for whom I have a great deal of regard and appreciation. They inspire me, and I hope they will do the same for you.

All these leaders have different lived experiences than my own. One of the most thought-provoking aspects of this book is that of sharing their experiences with great respect and humility. Some leaders are very public-facing and I do not want to speak out of turn or present their story other than how they shared it with me and how they intended it. Some shared more about their upbringing and journey than others.

You will see that I connect their stories with public-facing biographies and news stories or articles about them and their leadership. I will highlight their podcasts, books, articles, and/or social media postings. I have asked all the interviewees to read this book before submission to the publisher so that if I misrepresented their experiences, there would be time to make appropriate changes. For transparency's sake, some Leaders suggested edits, and others did not. I am grateful for their time and energy in being interviewed, reading this book, and making thoughtful edits.

While I know them all to be amazing people in their personal lives, I want to focus the majority of my sharing their stories on their professional leadership contributions. One of the key premises of this book is that there is a dearth of stories about Gen X leadership and our impact. I also want to focus on conveying their sage advice to you, as they have been a great resource and comfort to me through the years.

The Gen X leaders highlighted in this book are college leaders, philanthropic leaders, entrepreneurial business owners, and community and business leaders. They are racially and ethnically diverse, living across the country and working in urban, rural, and suburban communities. They have aging parents and Gen Z children. They have lost loved ones during the pandemic and experienced their own health challenges, all while managing colleges, businesses, and non-profit organizations during the multiple crises, including a tragic accident, political unrest, and the COVID-19 pandemic. I hope that you see some of your own story in theirs and that you can validate your own leadership and be inspired for your path forward.

Let's quickly meet our profiled Gen X leaders whom we'll spend some additional time with later in the book:

Dr. Warren Brown is a philanthropic leader, a former community college president leading a college through a nationally profiled crisis, a father, and a community leader.

The Honorable Victoria Woodards is a government and community leader, public servant, and organizer.

Dr. Julie Pham is a business owner, entrepreneur, author, newspaper leader, tech leader, and daughter of immigrant parents.

Andrea Heuston is a business owner, entrepreneur, author of *Lead Like a Woman*, podcaster, and mother.

Dr. William Serrata is a nationally recognized community college leader during the pandemic, and a father.

How This Book Is Structured

Gleaning lessons from their experiences and wisdom combined with my own experience as a long-term college president, leading my college through twin crises (the Great Recession and COVID-19), I'll share ways to prepare ourselves and those whom we lead to build our bridge to the future we all want to see. I'll do so in six pragmatic steps you can apply to your work and life today. Together, we'll learn to:

- Create the organizations we wanted at the beginning of our careers
- Nurture a community of Gen X leaders
- Stay curious and not let the grind grind us down
- Build the bench while calling the shots
- Call on Gen Z to join us and be the future we need
- Call in our Boomer retirees for coaching, mentoring, and support

This book is inspired by and designed for very busy Gen X leaders at all levels of all organizations. Like us, it is approachable, pragmatic, humble, and meant to be picked up and read in short segments—during a high school swim meet, while waiting for parents at a doctor's appointment, during a brief lunch break at your desk, or at the end of your day before you fall asleep tired from your heaping full plate of responsibilities.

I also developed a set of reflection questions at the end of every part of this book to walk you through steps you can take to prepare yourself and your organization for the future. I hope you will take each story and chapter and jot down a few notes about what has inspired you and how you can apply these lessons in your life.

In addition, I've developed a summary of Action Steps at the end of many of the chapters to highlight some of the lessons learned from each Gen X Leader and some questions for you to consider. You may want to grab a notebook and a pen. Also, you have my permission to jot notes down in this book along the way. So let's roll up our flannel shirt sleeves, grab that proverbial broom, gather your teams, and get to work.

Source: Getty Images, XiaoYun Li

PART I

Acknowledging the Leadership Crisis That We Are Now In

Chapter One

Our Boomer-Lined Path
to Leadership

Like many Gen X leaders, we spent the foundational years of our careers as the younger, junior, associate, and assistant leaders to Boomer bosses. For most of our careers, we were mentored by a few Traditionalists, but mostly Boomers, and were surrounded by Boomer colleagues. As a director in my late twenties, I distinctly remember suiting up for executive team meetings with my Boomer college president and colleagues. I was ready to make sure my department had what it needed and that I could convince my senior colleagues to help support my requests. I was the outlier, the youngest in the room, the kid sister of colleagues, to be sure.

To this day, many of my closest personal and professional friends and colleagues are Boomers. My husband is very much a Boomer. In fact, as I pause to think about it, my world and that of Gen X was completely shaped by Boomers. If you want to dive deep into the outsized influence of the Boomer generation on our country, you might want to check out the book *Aftermath: The Last Days of the Baby Boom and the Future of Power in America* by Philip Bump,[1] a columnist with the *Washington Post*. It's important to note that Bump self-identifies as a Gen Xer.

This way of working, surrounded by Boomers, our only known workplace dynamic, began to incrementally change around 2010. As a vice-president, my direct reports were younger, many of them younger Gen Xers or *Geriatric Millennials* (one of my favorite generational terms).[2] They were talented, driven, with young families, and ready to blaze a trail.

Around this time, in my own career, the remaining Traditionalists and early Boomers began to retire as The Great Recession wore on. Multiple years of deep cuts to our community and technical colleges, combined with increased student enrollments and workloads, signaled the end of an era for the older Boomers—a very long, growth-oriented, and frankly more exciting era for these founding community college leaders. Those of us remaining did double and triple duty to keep our doors open during the long tail of The Great Recession.

In 2013, as I started my term as president of Lake Washington Institute of Technology (LWTech), the college's workforce was largely comprised of Boomers, Gen Xers, and some Millennials. Then, nearly all my presidential colleagues were Boomers. In fact, I distinctly remember when Dr. Warren Brown (interviewed for this book) was hired as president of North Seattle College, and I thought to myself, *Wow, we now have four Gen X presidents; this is huge!*

I sat down for coffee with Dr. William Serrata in 2014. We were both new presidents with young families, at the beginning of what seemed like a very long career with infinite possibilities. We met at a national community college meeting, and I thought, *I finally found another Gen X leader; this is fantastic!* There were so few of us, and I felt a bit like a unicorn, a few Gen Xers completely surrounded by Boomers. William and I talked about our young families, our colleges, our hopes, and our challenges.

Looking back on that conversation, I think if you had told us then that a decade later we would be senior presidents, our colleagues would retire *en masse*, and, oh, by the way, there would be a global pandemic and a racial reckoning that we would be leading our colleges through, we probably would have looked at you askance and in typical Gen X fashion, shrugged our shoulders and got back to our conversation.

In the past decade, over 100 presidents and chancellors—acting, interim, and permanent—have transitioned in and out of 37 leadership positions in Washington State's community and technical college system. I felt this dizzying change on a visceral level, especially following the acute phase of the pandemic throughout 2022, when many of my colleagues and friends, upon whom I had depended for years, announced their retirements and exited stage left.

It wasn't until I took a bit of time to go through the list of presidents to count who had come and gone that I was able to articulate and verbalize this extensive turnover and wrap my mind around this pace of change (I wasn't the only one who tried to make sense of this change numerically; William went through the same exercise as I did). This turnover was, of course, accelerated by the pandemic when, as I mentioned, nearly 100 years of executive leadership left our system in 2022. I cannot or do not blame my colleagues for retiring; they have earned it, but goodness, did they have to leave all at once?

Chapter Two

Boomers Exit

THE FALLOUT

During the Spring and Summer of 2022, I started to wrestle with this pace and scope of leadership turnover and transition. Colleagues I have turned to, leaned on, and assumed would always be there were suddenly counting down the days until retirement and sending me save-the-date invitations to their retirement parties. Leaders, attorneys, and colleagues who for years held the keys to solving complex problems were suddenly at the center of Zoom screens, hearing proclamations read in honor of their thirty and forty years of service.

Time and time again, saying goodbye felt very uneasy, and I thought, *Who will answer my questions now? Who will I go to when the rubber hits the road? Who will hold the institutional memory regarding how we have conducted ourselves in the past?* And I know I am not the only one who felt the impacts of this seemingly dramatic and sudden shift.

It goes without saying that after the last couple of years, not all Boomers are retiring of their own volition, happily skipping out the door to a lifelong retirement party. Many lost their jobs after the early pandemic economic fallout; many were impacted by COVID-19. Unfortunately, many lost their lives to COVID-19. They cared for parents and grandchildren. And some suffer from the maddening and baffling symptoms of long COVID. In his November 30, 2022, address, the Chairman of the Federal Reserve, Jerome Powell, spoke extensively about the pandemic's impact on the Boomer generation:

> Some of the participation gap reflects workers who are still out of the labor force because they are sick with COVID-19 or continue to suffer lingering symptoms from previous COVID . . . what would have been expected from population

aging alone . . . might now account for more than 2 million of the 3 1/2 million shortfall in the labor force . . . the data so far do not suggest that excess retirements are likely to unwind because of retirees returning to the labor force. Older workers are still retiring at higher rates, and retirees do not appear to be returning to the labor force in sufficient numbers to meaningfully reduce the total number of excess retirees.[1]

This is a stark reminder that all generations were dramatically impacted by the pandemic on many levels and many Boomers did not choose their retirement path or its conditions.

Leading through a Sea of Grief and Loss

As leaders, during this time, we are all wrestling with the underlying grief and loss that is showing up in our workplaces. Our country has lost 1.5 million Americans to COVID since early 2020, and as of winter 2023, hundreds are still dying every day. Some were shocked when, in the same November 30, 2022 speech, Chairman of the Federal Reserve Jerome Powell attributed some of the dynamics of a strong and tight job market to not only The Great Resignation but the fact that over 500,000 working-aged Americans lost their lives to COVID. This is another heartbreaking reminder that the COVID-19 pandemic has impacted all of us in ways that are difficult to articulate. These impacts certainly play out in our organizations and compound already daunting workplace pressures for leaders.

Honestly, I am not sure we, individually or collectively, have come to terms with the magnitude of all we lost due to the COVID-19 pandemic. It may be the children or grandchildren of Gen Z who will finally be able to gain some perspective on the fallout and magnitude of our loss of human life and all the possibilities and opportunities lost. Simply put, as leaders right now we may not know or fully comprehend what grief and loss our colleagues, customers, friends, and loved ones are wrestling with and how it is impacting them. I hope, for all our sakes, that we are taking time to comprehend our own losses so that we may be better able to lead now and into the foreseeable future.

Losing Our Safety Net

Loss looks very different in the workplace as Boomers retire. I am not the only one who noticed and felt this generational shift. Dr. Julie Pham said that while she primarily works with younger colleagues in her current role as CEO and founder of CuriosityBased, she very much noticed the impact of this demographic change among her parents' generation and the stewardship of the Vietnamese American community in Seattle. She learned so much from her elders and shared stress and workload with them. "It felt a bit scary and looked different."

Julie shared that growing up in the United States, she was encouraged by her parents (owners of the Vietnamese community newspaper, *Northwest Vietnamese News*) and others to assimilate and not learn Vietnamese. She shared that a lot of institutional memory was lost with community newspaper leaders retiring, especially since so many had been leading since the 1990s.

Julie shared a beautiful tribute to her father upon his passing in 2021, published in the *Northwest Vietnamese News*.[2] She shared one interaction that underscored not only the importance of encouragement from her Boomer father, but also the passing of his entrepreneurial spirit to her. She writes,

> When I told my father, Kim Pham, I was going to leave my executive job at a remarkable nonprofit to start my own company in the middle of a pandemic, I was worried that he would disapprove or at the very least, warn me against it. Instead, he said, "I'm so happy for you. By having your own business, you are in control and you will have freedom." Spoken like the true entrepreneur that he was.

What a beautiful tribute to the personal and professional safety net the Boomer generation provided us.

Still others were impacted by having to rebuild their teams. Dr. William Serrata shared that he is doing something that never even occurred to him earlier in his career: he is now rebuilding his leadership team due to the retirements of his own executive team members whom he hired. Generational churn is all around with not only the turnover of his team, but with his governing board, as only a few members who originally hired him remain. And there are very few presidential colleagues left who were present when he started as president in 2012.

Andrea Heuston shared that she saw the Boomer retirement exodus coming, which impacted her team, and she lost many of her clients who retired from their companies. With the forthcoming retirement of her long-time creative director and other retirements, Andrea felt like she lost her professional "safety net." So, she created an employee emeritus program to keep Boomer employees partially engaged as they transition into retirement. Andrea aptly summed up what the mass Boomer exodus felt like as she shared the loss of the Boomer work ethic, perspective, knowledge, and connections: it felt like some of the "magic" was lost.

I can certainly relate to the feeling of a lost safety net, and I was at that point with so much turnover in 2022. With so many retirements in the pipeline a few of my Gen X colleagues and I waved the flag of surrender and said we needed some help with this coming transition. We're still working through this transition and new leader onboarding. I know our system is not the only one experiencing such dramatic and sudden changes in generational leadership, with Gen X leaders stepping in to fill substantial leadership voids within their organizations—it's one of the reasons why I wrote this book.

Pragmatic Leaders in a Time of Demanding Change

I am not the only Gen Xer who is now feeling the pressure of leading through the pandemic to a post-pandemic reality (still yet to be determined), as well as the added pressure of serving as the keeper of the flame, institutional historian, senior leader, the dean, the elder, and/or the adult in the room.

While I am working and leading through this transition, I am mindful of the fact that too much foreboding of our retired Boomers has the unintended consequence of making new colleagues, many of them fellow Gen X and Millennials, feel unwelcomed and unappreciated. Now more than ever, we need our new colleagues for their contributions and energy and for seeing us and our work with fresh eyes. Now is the time to be more mindful and welcoming of newer colleagues, joining from all points around the country, and all ages, stages, and lived experiences.

Moreover, while serving as a senior leader, we are called upon during this time to change and disrupt the systems that we inherited. This is not easy for Gen X. Dr. Warren Brown summed up the Gen X approach to changing structures that no longer served us with "a very pragmatic approach of changing them with good intentions." And now, for very good reasons, Millennials, and especially Gen Z, demand structural changes. Warren noted that currently, policy work has moved toward "focusing its purpose, its impact, and ways to change policy with movement toward equity." The pace and approach to balancing our more pragmatic approach to change with younger generations' demands for immediate systemic change remains a challenge with which we, as Gen X leaders, will continue to wrestle.

Building Bridges While Shaping Our Future

As we rise to this challenge, we must be more inclusive, equitable, and supportive of new leadership. This is the essential challenge of Gen X leadership: to build a bridge from the Boomer-led systems and structures to a Gen Z-centered future while making that bridge wider, more accessible, and leading us to a very different world from the one in which we grew up.

Currently, I am preparing my college for the third presidential election since I was hired as college president in 2013. As you can appreciate, supporting and leading a college community through the 2016 and 2020 presidential elections was anything but easy. In fact, I read recently that incidents of hate increased during presidential election years (*USA Today* article).[3] During these times, I have reflected on Dr. Margaret Wheatley's description of "Islands of Sanity"[4] and how, during national and international times of strife and division, we can create local, and at times hyperlocal, communities that support each other with respect and civility.

While we are tasked professionally with leading our diverse organizations through times of unprecedented external political division, we are challenged to do so personally, often caring for our children and parents while managing our own health challenges and, at the very least, trying to stay healthy physically and mentally. This challenge of midlife leadership is compounded by the fact that, as leaders, we are also expected to show up day after day for *others*. No one wants their boss to show up to work stressed, grumpy, and looking like their hair is on fire (figuratively, of course). I have near-daily conversations with midlife leaders who are reaching incredible heights in their careers while fielding medical calls for their ill parents and calls from school.

This substantial transition from how we have been used to operating for twenty-plus years of our career to a new and yet undefined future that we are seemingly in charge of is a heady experience. And like much of our lives as one of the smallest generations, no one really wants to hear us complain, if we are even acknowledged at all for our contributions to date and in the future.

Chapter Three

Ready or Not, We Are Now
the Adults in the Room

Gen X: we are now the adults in the room. If you are a fellow Gen Xer reading this book, together we can have a chuckle for a moment about this sentiment. For the majority of our lives, our generation was painted as disengaged, lazy, or worst of all, demographically insignificant due to our small size and generational zeitgeist. And yet, in many ways, we are exactly the generation to build a bridge to a better future for our younger colleagues and children.

We are the generation that was intentionally (or not) raised to be independent, self-motivated, and self-entertained. With the help and inspiration of Marlo Thomas, we were *Free to Be You and Me*. Thomas, in her lovely voice, sang to us all.

> To a land where the children are free
> And you and me are free to be
> And you and me are free to be
> And you and me are free to be you and me.[1]

Indeed, we enjoyed a great deal of freedom. We rode our bikes until dusk; we were latchkey kids who knew how to fend for ourselves and get our homework done without a hovering parent. Our parents did not even see our grades until they were final and mailed home, if then.

By all accounts, we kept our heads together during the pandemic, as tough as it was on everyone. And perhaps the fact that our generation was overshadowed by the size of the Boomers and, to a large degree, the Millennial generation, we have always worked in the in-between space, preparing us to be the pragmatic bridge builders we are today. Case in point: as of 2021, Boomers comprised 21.1 percent (70.2 million) of the US population, Millennials comprised 20.5 percent (67.9 million), Gen Z comprised 23 percent (75.9M), and Gen X, of course, the smallest of generational cohorts is approximately 18.5 percent of the US population (61.4 million) (Twenge, 2023).[2]

We find ourselves at a time once again when we are on our own. No one prepared us generationally to call the shots and become the elders seemingly overnight. I have been reflecting a great deal on this challenge. How do we embrace this role of senior leader? Who do we look to as Gen X leaders nationally and internationally? We can all quickly think of Boomer leaders—past presidents, business leaders, and philanthropic leaders. There are many high-profile and successful such leaders. And then conversely on the Millennial side, Silicon Valley business leaders, political upstarts, etc. We envision them with hoodies and a social media-fueled bully pulpit.

And what about national Gen X leaders? Who comes to mind to help us role model how to move forward during such a tumultuous time? There are a few high-profile business/high-tech leaders who come to mind. Although recently, Elon Musk comes to mind as he renamed Twitter X. It's hard to miss the black and white X where the blue bird used to chirp. Certainly, there are a number of high-profile Gen X entertainment leaders. Others? This was a more time-consuming exercise than brainstorming Boomer/Millennial leaders.

Insight and Inspiration from Gen X Leaders

While there might not be a glaring national spotlight on Gen X leadership, I am confident that you can name many Gen X leaders in your own world. Midlife peer leaders, colleagues, religious leaders, coaches, educational leaders, and local political leaders. Gen X leaders are impacting all aspects of our society without the fanfare of larger generational cohorts. We are one of the smallest generations, best known perhaps for being in between Boomers and Millennials. And right now, that's exactly the point.

I wrote this book so fellow Gen X leaders can see themselves and be inspired by those of us leading with pragmatism and in many ways without much credit. One of my goals throughout this book is to spotlight the often humble, behind-the-scenes, and under-appreciated Gen X leaders.

I also hope that by looking closely at Gen X leadership, we can gain insight and inspiration as to how we, as Gen X leaders, support Millennials and Gen Z as we move toward a truly multigenerational future. And as if it isn't challenging enough to become senior leaders almost overnight, we are doing so arguably during one of the most complex times to lead an organization of any size. Leadership challenges are significant, and our list of unanswered questions and worries is seemingly endless. Here are just a few of the questions on the minds of our Gen X leaders:

- When will the pandemic truly end? What will the post-pandemic norm really look like? Are we "there" now?

- How do I recruit, retain, and engage a multigenerational workforce that keeps everyone working in ways that suit them best while still meeting customer needs?
- How do I create an inclusive and equitable workplace during a divisive and polarizing time?
- How do I ensure my workplace and employees are safe from physical and cyber threats?
- How do I build a bench of future leadership when current leaders are tired from the pandemic?
- Am I already too old for this leadership role? Have the Millennials passed me by? Are Gen Zers the ones who are *really* in charge, with their demands for workplace change?
- How can I make my organization as resilient as possible given the many uncertainties in the world, from financial crises to climate crises?
- Finally, how can I paint a positive future outlook for my employees when the nightly news is chock full of violence, crisis, and political division?

Making Meaning in a Time of Uncertainty

It is my job in many ways as a leader and a leader of a workforce-oriented college to think about the workplace. My job is to ensure our students are prepared for success when they graduate and enter the workforce. It is also my responsibility to make sure that my employees are supported and successful as well. I pay close attention to future-oriented trends and try to align the work of the college when there is congruence with such trends.

After the past couple of years, I have been on an additional search for those who can make meaning out of our current environment and do so with integrity. Those who can put into words what I am seeing, sensing, and wrestling with. This is why I refer to a number of books, podcasts, articles, and audiobooks. Like you, I have many questions about how to lead my workplace and prepare our students for an uncertain future.

While this book will not be able to address all these questions and many other leadership worries, we're going to spend some time with Gen X leaders who will help illuminate paths forward during this time of incredible transition. I've had the privilege of knowing and working with them for many years. Their insight and experiences are equal parts inspiring and impactful. I am so honored and feel an immense amount of privilege to share their stories, and I strive to share their stories respectfully and appropriately.

Finally, by tapping into the experience, insight, and lessons from the leaders interviewed and combined with my own experiences, I will share six steps for building our bridge to a future that we all want and one in which we are uniquely suited to build. Being the pragmatic Gen Xer, educated by thick standard textbooks with my own new accompanying workbook at the start of every school year (what Gen Xer doesn't love a workbook?), I strongly encourage you to grab your own notebook or planner so that you can develop your own sanity-saving, bridge-building plan while reading this book.

Like it or not, this is our time to step forward and ensure that we build a metaphorical bridge to a better future for our organizations and future generations. We may never get appropriate credit for moving forward, and that is okay. We will have to give ourselves a proverbial gold star because whether they know it or not, Boomers, Millennials, and especially our children's Generation Z, needs us now more than ever.

GEN X LEADERSHIP REFLECTION QUESTIONS

1. When was the first time you realized you were the youngest in the room, surrounded by Boomer leaders?
2. Who were your Boomer mentors? Colleagues? Friends?
3. When was the first time you realized Millennial coworkers were on the scene? When did you hire your first Gen Xer, Millennial, and Gen Z?
4. When did you realize that you were in charge? That you were the senior leader? That you were the keeper of institutional memory and upholder of organizational culture?
5. What expectations are you now facing—internal and external—as the senior leader or the leader with seniority?
6. What is keeping you up at night in your leadership role?

ACTION STEPS: FULLY ACKNOWLEDGE THE LEADERSHIP CRISIS WE ARE NOW IN

Appreciate our generation and where we are today. No other generational cohort of living memory has grown up between two such large, impactful, and very different generational cohorts. Arguably, Gen X is more aware of this dynamic because we never grew up nor have come into midlife surrounded completely by contemporaries of the same age and stage. This is a different awareness that is not shared by Boomers and most likely not as much with Millennials. Check out *The Aftermath: The Last Days of The Baby Boom and the Future of Power in America* by Philip Bump (who is Gen X) for an in-depth understanding of the role the Boomer generation has played in our nation and upon Gen X.

Accept Boomer retirements. Boomers are retiring and ready or not, we are now in charge with Millennial colleagues and Gen Z rising. Comfortable or not, that is now our reality, and bemoaning how things used to be and how we used to do things is not serving anyone or making our newer colleagues feel welcome.

We have a lot of work to do. We have no shortage of work to do right now, shoring up our families, communities, businesses, and organizations post-pandemic. We are in charge and no one wants to hear us whine. Fortunately, we are not whiners. We have always been independent and able to work in between more vocal and, frankly, more demanding generations. For a comprehensive account of why our generation, in particular, is squeezed tight in midlife, check out *Why We Can't Sleep: Women's New Midlife Crisis*, by Ada Calhoun[3] or *Overwhelmed: Work, Love, and Play When No One Has the Time*, by Brigid Schulte.[4]

Remains of COVID grief and loss. Grief and loss following the pandemic are going to be with us for a long time and will look different with each generation and individual. Take some time to understand and heal as you can your own grief so that you are able to lead others. I think one of the foremost speakers on how we move through disasters and make meaning and frankly sense of what we are going through is Dr. Kira Mauseth. I encourage you to find her many presentations on YouTube. Her lectures on compassion fatigue, burnout, and moral injury are particularly impactful as we navigate our way through a post-pandemic world.[5] I have invited Dr. Mauseth to speak to my colleagues multiple times through the pandemic. You can connect with her through her website at Astrum Health.

Source: Getty Images, XiaoYun Li

PART II

Lessons from Gen X Leadership

Chapter Four

Setting the Stage for How Gen X Leaders Pick Up the Post-Pandemic Pieces and Move Forward

One of the great joys of writing this book was spending focused time with Gen X leaders whom I've admired for many years. They are public, private, entrepreneurial, non-profit, local, state, and nationally recognized leaders. They are parents and caregivers to their parents. They are diverse in many ways: gender, race, marital status, and demographics. They are leaders in areas of equity and social justice, children of immigrants, educators, and working parents. They were latchkey kids and often responsible for younger siblings. The music from the 1980s and 1990s played an essential role in their upbringing. Some faced health challenges. All faced substantial leadership challenges before, during, and after the pandemic. All continue to lead today. They inspire me to continue my work, and I believe they will do the same for you.

You may ask how I decided on which Gen X leaders to interview for this book. How did I come to know them? Up close and from afar, I have crisscrossed professional and personal paths with all of them in my twenty-four years in the community and technical college system.

APPROACHING LEADERS WITH CULTURAL HUMILITY

At this point, I do want to explicitly acknowledge that I am a middle-aged, straight, cisgender white woman who grew up in a working-class family in the Pacific Northwest. In some ways, my leadership path intersects with those I have interviewed. In other ways, my path to leadership, upbringing, and how I live my life now differs from those I've interviewed. I am incredibly grateful to those interviewed in this book for sharing their stories about their upbringing, their path to leadership, and their leadership challenges. I interviewed these leaders with the utmost regard and care and within a lens of *Cultural Humility.*

Cultural Humility is a framework developed by health care practitioners Melanie Tervalon and Jann Murray-García. They developed this framework to serve their diverse patients better. We have adopted their framework at our college when working with our students, who are diverse in many ways. Tervalon and Murray-García define Cultural Humility as,

> the ability to practice lifelong learning and critical self-reflection in order to understand one's own cultural identity and its impact on being open to and supporting the cultures of others . . . it is different from cultural competence because it focuses on self-humility rather than achieving a state of awareness or expertise, particularly of a culture to which one does not belong.[1]

It is with a heaping dose of humility that I convey these stories of leadership in this book with the utmost respect, regard, and care. While I know all of the leaders (in real life, that is), I am self-aware enough to know that I do not fully understand the personal lens through which they view the world. Their stories are robust enough to fill their own books. Indeed, some of them have, and I have referenced their works in the endnotes. The bottom line is that through the lens of Cultural Humility, while I have strived to tell their stories as they would like to be told, I do so with a profound appreciation that there is always more to learn and understand.

I am also grateful to work with a college community that continuously reflects upon how we can better support students and our fellow employees. Since 2013, and especially following the election of 2016 and the summer of 2020, my college community has been in a period of substantial reflection and transformation, especially regarding diversity, equity, and inclusion (DEI). We are working to ensure that all our students are prepared to succeed in their chosen educational and career pathways, understand what DEI looks like in their chosen fields, and approach their future careers through a lens of Cultural Humility.

Leaders and "leaders"

For the sake of transparency, while I have known each of these Leaders for many years, for the purposes of this book, I spent a full hour interviewing each of them formally. Prior to sending the final draft of the book to the publisher, I asked each of the Leaders to make sure that they were completely comfortable with all that I shared in this book and how I conveyed their stories, and I gave them full editing rights.

My hope for this work is that our stories are of comfort during this challenging time of incredible transition and ultimately inspiring so that you as a Gen X leader know you are not alone in your work. I have received a great deal of support and inspiration from these Leaders, and I hope you will feel the same.

Throughout this book, I have incorporated references to some of the Leaders' toughest and most exemplary times of leadership through news articles, podcast links, website links, book links, etc. I hope that if there is a Leader whose experiences particularly speak to you that you will have the opportunity to engage with them and their broader work. If you would like to reach out to them to make a business connection, buy their books, and/or learn more about their stories, there is an opportunity to do so. While all these Leaders were very generous with their time and spirit in sharing their stories, they did so with the broader intention of supporting other leaders.

Also, for the purposes of this book, I will refer to the Leaders who are interviewed as the *Leaders.* When I refer generally to a Gen X *leader*, I will not be referring to those interviewed in this book. With that said, I consider leaders in general with a broad scope. Leadership occurs not only at the CEO, president, or vice-president levels but at all levels of all organizations. Leaders are managers, coordinators, and/or subject matter experts who have an outsized influence wherever they may be within their organizational structure. Leaders are also entrepreneurs of organizations of all sizes, and certainly volunteers are leaders as well. If you are reading this, congratulations; you are a leader in your professional and/or personal life.

Chapter Five

Profiles in Gen X Leadership

For the purposes of this book, I interviewed the following Gen X Leaders, some of whom you have already heard about in chapter 1. However, for ease of future reference, let me formally introduce them to you. Again, when I refer to them as a group, I will refer to them as the *Leaders*; when I refer to them individually, I will refer to them by their first name. I want to make sure they are recognized for their excellence in scholarship, business, and service, which is why I list their formal titles below. They are listed here in alphabetical order and their official biographies are referenced. Photographs of each Leader have been taken from their official biographies. All Leaders are also on LinkedIn.

Dr. Warren Brown has served as the executive director of the College Spark Foundation Washington State since 2020. Warren is an incredible leader who has transformed College Spark into an equity-centered philanthropic organization. Prior to his current role, Warren led North Seattle College during the tragic accident that killed five international students and injured over forty staff and students when their tour bus collided with a Duck Boat in Seattle. Prior to his leadership role at North Seattle, he served as a professor and administrator, developing partnerships with various school districts, nonprofit organizations, universities, and community colleges. He holds a master's degree in nonprofit administration and a doctorate in education focusing on improving higher education curriculum and instruction, with an emphasis on educational technologies and multicultural curriculum development.

As a colleague, I have had the delightful opportunity to witness Warren as supportive husband and engaged father. As a reflection of his commitment to his family, his official biography notes, Warren . . . "has a daughter and a son, who constantly keep him on his toes, while also showing him the simple and beautiful things in life that are often missed by adults."

Andrea Heuston is the CEO of Artitudes Design, a company she founded over twenty years ago. She is an entrepreneur, business leader, author of multiple editions of *Lead Like a Woman*[1] and the founder of a podcast by

Dr. Warren Brown
Source: College Spark WA

the same name. Andrea is perhaps best known as a strong advocate and supporter of women leaders and entrepreneurs. Andrea is an active member of the Women's Business Enterprise Council (WBEC) and Entrepreneurs' Organization (EO).

Her weekly podcast, *Lead Like a Woman*, enjoys a devoted following and inspires women to overcome social and cultural trappings to become their best selves (I also had the privilege of being interviewed on her podcast). Her LinkedIn article, "Never Apologize for Being a Strong Woman" attracted over a million readers in a single month. Andrea is also well known for her magnetic personality. Her professional biography notes that she is "authentic, unapologetic, curious, stubborn, empathetic, and always ready to laugh and learn. Clients and employees alike turn to her for inspiration and advice,

Andrea Heuston
Source: Artitudes

drawing on a wealth of knowledge and experience gained from thirty years in design, tech, and leadership."

If you want to know more about Andrea, her success story was chronicled in her best-selling memoir, *Stronger on the Other Side*. Andrea is also a mother of two adult sons, and she has two dogs. We traded many stories through the years while raising our now-adult sons.

Dr. William Serrata has served as the president of El Paso Community College in El Paso, Texas, since August 2012. William is locally, regionally, and nationally recognized as a student success leader with an emphasis on first-generation and Hispanic populations while establishing a college-going culture.

William holds a bachelor's degree from Texas A&M University-College Station, a master's degree from the University of Texas at Brownsville,

Dr. William Serrata
Source: El Paso Community College

and a PhD in educational human resource development from Texas A&M University-College Station.

William's full biography connotes extensive leadership commitment and recognition. To name a few of his contributions, he is an active member of the El Paso community and currently serves as the chair of the El Paso Collaborative for Academic Excellence and serves on the board of directors for the El Paso branch of the Federal Reserve Bank of Dallas.

At the state level, William serves as the Texas Association of Community Colleges (TACC) chair. On the national level, he serves on the board of directors for the Lumina Foundation and has previously served as chair of the board of directors for the American Association of Community Colleges (AACC).

Under William's leadership, the Aspen Institute announced that El Paso Community College (EPCC) was named one of ten nationwide finalists for the 2015 Aspen Prize for community college excellence, which recognizes a college's impact on student success. I encourage you to read his official biography to get a full scope of his excellence in leadership.[2] He is also a dedicated husband and a father.

Dr. Julie Pham is the Founder and CEO of CuriosityBased. She notes in her official bio that she leveraged

> 15+ years of community-organizing, including building a cross-sector collaboration for the tech industry, founding an ethnic media coalition, running a Vietnamese-language newspaper, and mobilizing small business owners in South Seattle, combined with 8 years of academic research, to start this consulting practice focused on fostering curiosity, collaboration, and inclusion in the workplace.[3]

I had the good fortune of meeting Julie as she created and led the Ion Collaborators Program at the Washington Technology Industry Association (where I served on the board). I also had the good fortune of participating in Julie's company's workshop at my college and at one of the signings for her book, *7 Forms of Respect*.[4]

While I have called upon Julie and her colleagues for DEI expertise and engagement at my college, she writes in her official company biography:

Dr. Julie Pham
Source: Curiosity Based

My approach to belonging and inclusion has been informed by having lived as an expatriate in Asia and Europe and having grown up as a refugee in the US. Though I don't consider myself a DEI expert, I have deep experience in motivating people from diverse personal and professional backgrounds to connect and collaborate.

I encourage you to check out Julie's official biography and the CuriosityBased website for additional information and inspiration.

The Honorable Victoria Woodards has been the Mayor of Tacoma, Washington since 2018. She is a public servant *extraordinaire*, community builder, and leader. She is a self-identified Army brat, an Army veteran herself, and past executive director of the Tacoma Urban League, director for the Tacoma Rainiers Baseball Club, and a former Tacoma City Council member.

Mayor Victoria Woodards
Source: City of Tacoma (WA)

She is currently the president of the National League of Cities and is a national leader of many public policy initiatives, including affordable housing, public safety, immigrant and refugee support, youth, and even piloting guaranteed income. While a city council member, she launched the Equity and Empowerment initiative, which led to the establishment of the city's Office of Equity and Human Rights and brought partner organizations together for then-President Barack Obama's My Brother's Keeper initiative. With an unparalleled track record of community service and commitment to anti-racist policies, Mayor Woodards led her city successfully through the pandemic and the Racial Reckoning in the summer of 2020. I encourage you to read her full biography, as it is inspiring.[5]

Chapter Six

Gen X Childhoods and How They Framed Who We Are Today

THE ORIGINAL FREE-RANGE CHILDREN

If there is a throughline of how each of the Leaders came of age, it would include descriptors such as *latchkey kids*, *independent*, and *responsible* for watching younger siblings. No matter their parents' socioeconomic status or marital status, the Leaders were on the move and rose to their parents' expectations of caring for themselves after school. Many talked about the influence their parents' jobs had on their own career decision-making and specifically that of their mothers' jobs and careers. In Twenge's *Generations*, she notes that Gen X latchkey kids "didn't exist just because more mothers worked—they existed because schools and society were slow to recognize the new reality that most school children no longer had a stay-at-home parent" (p. 162).

Dr. Julie Pham self-identifies as a Gen Xer and latchkey kid. As a child of refugee parents, she also grew up taking care of her younger brothers. Julie recalls that there were limited options for after-school food, and she laughingly noted that she still doesn't like a lot of variety of food (I can also vividly recall the preferred choice of after-school snacks along with my brother—Life cereal was a particular hit). Julie's refugee parents started their own business, and she grew up in a Vietnamese refugee community where she was proud of her community. Hers was an entrepreneurial home where there was no shame in asking for help.

Julie also noted that there was an expectation within her Vietnamese American generation to assimilate. English was spoken to assimilate, and her diversity wasn't seen as an advantage then as it is now. She recognizes how much her parents did and how they and she had to figure things out together. She is proud of her and her family's strong sense of optimism, freedom, and

29

independence as political refugees, a sentiment that she said is "really easy to take for granted."

Andrea Heuston describes her upbringing as that of a quintessential Gen X latchkey kid: "I had a key around my neck at eight." She and her older brother ate *SpaghettiOs* and cookie dough after school and played with neighborhood kids while growing up in Washington and a few years in Canada. She spent her summer days outside, not watching television. Her parents were Traditionalists and gave her an allowance at age four for setting the table, and she was baking at age six. As a child, she had fun in her parent's rec room and as an '80s teen with a "lot of Aqua Net" (I, too, will confess to using quite a bit of hairspray from that iconic pink and white can). She recalls how music was so important to her and continues to be very important. She confesses to still exercising to all '80s music! No wonder Andrea has so much energy!

Her upbringing fostered a spirit of independence and resilience throughout her life. Andrea's independent spirit was honed when she was allowed to live in Denmark with a host family from age sixteen to seventeen. She moved out at eighteen and "never looked back." She reflected that she was afforded a lot of freedom as a child and tries to give that to her own children. Andrea says she tries hard "not to be a helicopter parent." I want to underscore that as a Gen X parent, that is easier said than done with our Gen Z children, especially as we come out of the pandemic.

Chapter Seven

Gen X Leadership Coming of Age

OPPORTUNITY FOR LEADERSHIP SKILL BUILDING AT A YOUNG AGE

Mayor Victoria Woodards was three when her family moved to Tacoma. Her mother was from England and her dad was in the military. Victoria described her childhood as growing up poor "but I didn't feel poor . . . we sat around the electric oven for heat and it felt like an adventure." Victoria grew up on grilled cheese sandwiches every night for dinner and she would often go visit her mom at the restaurant where she worked. They moved around a lot. A self-described Pollyanna, Victoria always saw the glass half full, and even when she looks back on her childhood now, she doesn't think it was a particularly hard one.

Mayor Victoria attributes the confidence and leadership skills she gained as a young woman to her church family in Tacoma, where she was the president of her youth group and where she sang in the choir. She was also involved in the high school Reserve Officers Training Corps (ROTC). Looking back, she was moving toward leadership at a very young age.

Living through Tremendous Social and Political Change

Dr. Warren Brown talked a lot about living through the late 1970s through the early 1990s, during a time of tremendous change that impacted our formative Gen X childhood experiences. We can all remember many of these global and societal shifts from Iran Contra, the Cold War, and the constant threat of nuclear war, tremendous policy and economic changes, as well as women and mothers going to work. At one point, Warren's dad was laid off from his job and his parents convened a family meeting. After that, Warren took on a paper route and learned the important lesson that jobs aren't permanent.

Warren's mother also returned to work when he was a little older, and he, too, found himself a latchkey kid with the added complication of the implementation of mandatory school busing. His parents eventually moved to the majority-white part of the Seattle School District so that he would not be bussed. Warren reflected that many, albeit well-intentioned, political and policy changes made during this time had real impacts on his life and that of his family. He noted that our generation's adult leaders' answer to improving those structures was to do so "with a very pragmatic approach of changing them with presumed good intentions." However, he reflected that "now many changes are geared toward equity and urgency," which Warren is leading through his philanthropic work.

I would add that the Reagan-era breaking of the air traffic controllers' union had a dramatic impact on my dad's life (as a card-carrying union member), and to this day, I believe that event and the worry it caused our family propelled me to get involved in politics and public policy as a young woman. Like Warren, I, too, wanted to change government from the inside to better mitigate the impacts on families like mine.

A few of the Leaders I interviewed spoke fondly of the impactful role that music played in their upbringing. Perhaps I am more attuned to this as well, having grown up in the greater Seattle area during the height of the grunge music scene. To this day, I remember my brother cranking up Aerosmith on our mother's wall stereo (as it took up nearly the entire wall) after she left for work and before we went to school. I can clearly remember the first days of MTV with Billy Idol sneering at me and telling my grandfather, "this is a big deal!" Warren also talked about MTV and the spotlight on Black artists— especially Michael Jackson. He noted that Black music culture was "where my jam was." For Warren, growing up, hip-hop and rap music were where he could see himself represented. Rap music, he reflects, also "led to the predominately white popular culture embracing Black pop culture."

In Hindsight, Growing Up in a Simpler Time

When I reflect upon my own upbringing as a true latchkey kid, with my brother and I at home while my mom and dad (divorced) both worked, I think about how dramatically different my upbringing was compared to my son's. Certainly, we did not live through a once-in-100-year pandemic. However, we did live through times of war and a constant threat of nuclear war (remember the chilling movie *Red Dawn*), and yet without pervasive technology and social media, it now seems like a much simpler time.

In hindsight, this upbringing gave us time and space to figure out who we were, who we wanted to be (other than everyone wanted to be Oprah, of course, me included), and the worst we seemingly could do after school was to catch the last few moments of a soap opera before the official "after-school" television programming began. No cell phones, no cable news, no social media, no viral videos, bullying yes, cyber bullying no. Mostly, we had the ability to be ourselves, as goofy as we were as teens, without fear of the whole world knowing about it.

Perhaps as we emerge from the pandemic, we are all a bit nostalgic for a simpler time. A time when kids could safely ride their bikes with friends, play recreational sports (without the pressure of having to play competitive sports to earn a college scholarship), be goofy, and mess up, and a time when our parents checked our grades only when they were mailed home after the term was over and they were final, if then.

Chapter Eight

Boomers

Our Teachers, Bosses, Coworkers, Mentors, and Friends

HOW THEY FRAMED OUR WORKING
LIVES AND OPPORTUNITIES

While Gen X children were defined by our independence, music, and, at times, less attractive descriptors (often aligned with unpleasant descriptions of grunge rock or rap music), we soon graduated, and many of us were the first in our families to go to college. I did, and it felt like a big deal. I was heading to college to realize my full potential and blaze a trail. To where, I wasn't quite sure, but a path toward some form of public service. Upon graduation, we were the "young guns" at work, often the youngest in the room, surrounded by mostly Boomer bosses and mentors.

The Youngest in the Room

While some of us were aware of our generation earlier due to the popular media defining us based on music labels or the *Time* magazine headlines trying to describe our generational zeitgeist, some of us didn't fully understand our generational place until we entered the workforce. Much like Dr. William Serrata, I, too, was always the youngest administrator in the room. We came of professional age surrounded completely by Boomers, supported by Boomer mentors and leaders, and aligning ourselves closely with the Boomer work ethic.

William noted that after college, he came home to Brownsville Community College as an enrollment analyst with a degree making $20,300. William then went to work for South Texas Community College to become a compliance specialist where the founding president believed you "didn't have to pay your dues" as a leader. From there, William rose through the student services ranks quickly to become a vice-president in less than a decade. Another Boomer leader encouraged William to take over the reins at El Paso Community College (EPCC), where he has been since 2012.

As Millennials came of age and entered the workforce, William noted that in many ways, Gen X, one of the smallest generations in recent history, seemed to get lost between the Boomers and the Millennials. He describes fellow Gen X leaders as those who "love what we do, and we work together to get things done."

That approach served William and EPCC well, as the college faced serious accreditation challenges early in his career. He addressed those challenges by 2014 and led EPCC to become an Aspen finalist in 2015 as one of the top 10 community colleges in the country and an American Association of Community College (AACC) student success award winner. While involved in multiple local boards, William was the chair of AACC in 2021, and the pandemic consumed his entire national chairmanship. I will say that I was quite saddened by the timing of William's national service as I believe he was the first Gen X AACC president, and I was cheering him on from the West Coast. That said, it was reassuring that he was in that role during a crisis.

Like William, I distinctly remember being the youngest in the room for years. I was full of energy and readiness to make my point, advocate for my department, and protect my department from cuts. While I was certainly aware of the difference in age and stage from my colleagues, for some reason, they not only tolerated me but welcomed me. They asked me for advice, appreciated my contributions, and became my friends. To this day, some of my most treasured friendships are with Boomers from early on in my career. I miss working with them but I am grateful that they are still in my life.

Boomer Mentors . . . Watch and Learn

Not surprisingly, many of the Leaders talked specifically about the role of their Boomer mentors, how they helped to create opportunities for them, convinced Gen Xers that they could take on important leadership roles, created space for them to learn to lead and eventually lead, by providing encouragement and examples. As I reflect upon the Leaders' experiences and that of my own, as Gen X leaders, we should keep these reflections in mind as we think about supporting Millennial and especially Gen Z leaders.

While I have tried to strike a balance of pandemic and post-pandemic workplace flexibility, I do wonder about how Gen Z colleagues will see and work with Gen X and Millennial mentors if we are not physically together, working side by side, day after day, year over year. I now have nearly thirty years in public service and all of that, except 2020 and part of 2021, have been full-time and in-person, or what came to be known during the pandemic as IRL (in real life). As with most aspects of leadership, I do think we need to acknowledge that while there is a great opportunity that comes with flexible work, we also need to be mindful of the opportunity cost, especially the opportunity to prepare Millennials and Gen Z for future leadership opportunities.

While many of the Leaders spoke fondly of their Boomer mentors, none touched me the way Mayor Victoria Woodards talked of her mentor and friend, the late Harold Moss, the thirty-fourth mayor of Tacoma, Washington. Harold was the first African American member of the city's council, its first African American mayor, and the first African American member of the Pierce County Council (I also had the very good fortune of knowing Harold). After honing her leadership skills in the military, she left the military and went to work with Harold Moss. She worked closely with Harold as his council aide.

Victoria thought at the time that this was her niche, standing by and right behind the seat of power and getting a lot of things done, even when there was a lot going around her. Then Harold and others encouraged her to serve on the Tacoma parks board. She continued her service to the community. Victoria said that serving on the parks board was a real shot in the arm to her self-esteem.

Mayor Victoria has a great definition of mentorship of Gen Xers by Boomers; she shared that then "mentorship meant people looked up to you . . . it wasn't formal or planned; it looked different than how it looks now." That said, her mentors, three prominent African American leaders in the Tacoma community, would "give their shirts off their back if you needed them." But, she noted, "they would expect you to *pay attention* and follow their lead." "They wanted to see your commitment to their mentorship," and for Victoria, their mentorship meant her ability to be side by side with her leaders and to watch them break new ground. She said she had worked so hard with them.

I also had the good fortune of two exceptional mentors at a very young age, the late State Senator Betti Sheldon and Congressman Norm Dicks. As a first-generation college graduate, I felt so fortunate to watch Senator Sheldon serve her constituents as the first cohort of women elected leaders after the 1992 election, dubbed *The Year of the Woman*. Betti was the consummate legislator and epitomized grace under fire; she donned a power suit like no woman I ever knew. I can remember like it was yesterday that when she was on her feet all day on the state senate floor, she would slip on red flats to match her red power suit. I was in awe, watched her every move, and observed closely how she interacted with constituents and legislators. Always present, always calm, always moving toward a pragmatic solution.

It was thanks to Betti that I had the incredible opportunity to work for Congressman Norm Dicks, a true force of nature, often referred to as Washington State's third senator. Like Victoria working alongside Harold Moss, I never worked harder than I did for Congressman Dicks, whom we all referred to as Norm. During evenings, weekends, events, speaking events, and then the campaign stint, I worked tirelessly for Norm, which is why congressional staff and campaign work are ideal for the young and unencumbered.

Fortunately, like Victoria, I had the opportunity to watch Norm in action and learn from his example, primarily that of understanding and serving one's diverse and demanding constituency. I cannot fully express my gratitude for these two exemplary public servants. The ability to watch and learn from them up close, through good times and challenging times, are lessons that have served me incredibly well as a technical college president where I often feel like the mayor of a small city with my own diverse and yes, at times, demanding constituency.

Creating One's Own Path (with Boomer Support)

There is also a thread of entrepreneurialism and self-reliance in the coming-of-age stories of the Leaders. I wonder about the independence expected of our generation at an early age, our latchkey childhoods, and how that upbringing shaped our careers and leadership roles. There is a common thread among the Leaders' employment paths of "this is not working for me any longer; I need to do something else" and then making a change. Sometimes, that meant moving to a different job or role, and for others, it meant creating their own business altogether. Those moves take incredible courage and a foundation of resilience and self-reliance.

I have often reflected on my personal journey and how different it was from my grandmother's and mother's. My generation was one of the first where girls and women were expected to go to college; work in successful careers; and succeed at home, school, sports, and life. Of course, we would be unable to do so without the trails blazed by Boomer women and those earlier achievers. And while these early expectations may have resulted in midlife complications and stressors, I am in awe of the fearlessness of the Leaders.

We Model Resilience with a Boomer Work Ethic

In her twenties, Dr. Julie Pham spent a lot of time on her PhD while managing the University of California academic journal on Vietnamese studies. She realized that she did not want to stay in academia as she was leading without authority, and she had to show deference to others without getting things done. So Julie came home to work with her father at the family newspaper.

Her parents encouraged her to take advantage of the flexibility of doing business in the United States so she and her brother purchased a stake in half the family newspaper. Julie ran the weekend edition and her parents ran the weekly edition of the *Northwest Vietnamese News*. Julie worked diligently on bringing in American corporate ads and left the paper without debt. She created a "real life MBA" by running the paper.

In addition, Julie was very involved with multicultural leadership with the Dr. Martin Luther King, Jr. Leadership Association and the multicultural newspaper coalition in Seattle. As the youngest person in the room, Julie was surrounded by eight leaders who spoke six different languages. Julie noted that her Vietnamese parents worked hard so their children didn't have to work in small business and community. She emphasized that expectation is changing now.

Both Julie and Mayor Victoria personify the many leadership aspects of community building that can also be applied to team building. Certainly, motivating volunteers is much like motivating employees to work across differences. They did so while balancing societal norms, even when, at times, that meant self-censorship as a woman of color. Julie reflects that one of the "gifts" of being a Vietnamese refugee and the gift of a "minority" is that she is always aware of who she is in relationship to others. And she references the famous 'be like water' quote from Bruce Lee:

> Empty your mind. Be formless. Shapeless. Like water. You put water into a cup, it becomes the cup. You put water into a bottle, it becomes the bottle. You put it in a teapot, it becomes the teapot. Water can flow, or it can crash. Be water, my friend.[1]

Julie notes that as Gen Xers, "we model resilience." Certainly, her career trajectory is defined by resilience within academia, the family newspaper, Big Tech, a statewide technology industry association (where we first met), and then starting her own company.

Julie takes away two key lessons from her career trajectory. The first is to be frugal with major changes to salary with different roles. That frugality has afforded her a lot of freedom in her career. Also, to do her own work in her own name, eventually as a full-time entrepreneur owning her own business. While she admits she had a lot of freedom in her role at the technology industry association, she appreciated that her dad supported her leaving that job. He told her that "freedom was never having the fear of losing her job (as an entrepreneur)." The many lessons that Julie learned from her father are lovingly summarized in the *Northwest Vietnamese News*.[2]

That freedom of never having the fear of losing your job is a hard lesson learned by many of our generation. Some Leaders' parents lost their jobs;

in my case, the threat of my own dad losing his union pension and health insurance was nerve-wracking as a young person. Honestly, I think that uncertainty at a tender age shaped my entire trajectory into a career in public service and advocacy.

Andrea Heuston began her career working in an engineering firm, and after eight years of working there, the firm was bought. She had to lay off her entire team, and then she was laid off! Two days later, she was asked to come back, and that was when she decided to launch her own business. Her former company was her first client (I love that story and have repeated it many times). Andrea's company, Artitudes, was formed. In case you are curious, the great name for her company originated from a conversation with her husband. She has owned Artitudes for twenty-seven years. It has grown and adapted substantially since that time.

Working around Boomer Barriers

While all the Leaders talk about Boomer role models, mentors, and bosses, there is also an acknowledgment that Boomers also put some serious roadblocks in our way. Dr. Warren Brown felt like much of his career had been spent balancing between showing older generations that he was ready and modeling for younger generations that there was always room to grow.

In his first full-time community college faculty position, a "stereotypical" Boomer department job chair told him, "This job is not easy work, and it's hard every day." He was asked to fit the Boomer "my way or the highway" ethos, which he felt could also be described as "our way or you're not a fit." These barriers, including the scuttling of a sabbatical opportunity, put Warren on a path at different colleges where he learned critical lessons about seeing both management and employee perspectives.

Warren eventually supervised basic and transitional studies alongside many Boomers and learned a lot from them. Warren learned to translate between faculty and administration and helped maneuver around the Boomer "my way or the highway" ethos. This ability to adapt over time and continue to do so led Warren to reflect that "I can remember a time when you could not bring your personal life to work and were told 'don't ask to telecommute.'" This ability to adapt early in our careers to the Boomer work ethos while eventually accommodating Millennial expectations as leaders led Warren to conclude that "we are the bridge generation." I couldn't agree more.

Calling in Boomer Reinforcements

One of the challenges multiple Leaders never thought they would find themselves in is being in the position of preparing to transition for the retirement of long-time, knowledgeable, and reliable Boomer colleagues. Dr. William Serrata mentioned that he is now preparing for the retirements and turnover of Boomer members of his executive team, something that he thought would never happen during his tenure.

I am preparing for the retirement of a Boomer colleague who is in a critical position. We're hiring far in advance of his retirement, hoping for the best and preparing for the worst—a failed search. I took a page from Andrea Heuston's playbook to offer this retiring Boomer an emeritus and/or part-time role, a brilliant move that has kept part of her safety net intact while preparing for the inevitable generational transition.

Another note on Gen X mentorship by the Boomers: we miss them. Leadership is lonely at the top. I have had some colleagues for whom I shed tears at their retirement. I treasured their friendship and counsel so much that I wondered if our monthly meetings as a system of college presidents would ever be the same. One of those dear colleagues is a friend and mentor, Dr. Jean Hernandez. She transitioned into retirement effortlessly (from my vantage point, at least), continuing to give back while a retiree as a college coach and, most excitedly for me, an interim president. As she transitions yet again into more full-time retirement, I am reassured that while I will miss seeing her regularly in professional settings, we will be in touch.

That said, there is nothing better than having a friend return from the land of retirement into an interim role. It's like putting on your favorite sweater and being welcomed by a feeling of familiarity, comfort, and safety. It feels like some of your professional safety net has been bolstered after so many Boomer retirements left it in tatters. My request to Boomer colleagues? Keep in touch, have lunch or coffee with us, and feel free to come back occasionally, even if it's only for a short-term gig.

Chapter Nine

Gen X's Profiles in Courage

LEADING THROUGH DIFFICULT
TIMES AND LESSONS LEARNED

This might be the part of the story of Gen X Leaders that really needs to be told. I have seen time and time again Gen X leaders step forward and take on the hard task without fanfare and accolades. I am eager to share and celebrate the unmistakable courage and resilience that these Leaders showed during some incredibly difficult professional times.

When I think about the leadership our Leaders have shown, especially through the pandemic, I reflect upon the words of professor and philosopher Dr. Margaret Wheatley,[1] who helped me make sense of a challenging time, 2016 (then 2020, etc.). Dr. Wheatley, in her pre-pandemic lecture to a group of college administrators, described the time in which we are now, where local leadership is stepping forward to reframe our communities and country, without the glare of the controversial national spotlight, with intention, with meaning, and in good faith attempting to create "Islands of Sanity" within their spheres of influence. I have so appreciated Dr. Wheatley's sage advice and strived for the past several years (with varying degrees of success) to create said Island of Sanity for my college, my community, my family, and, at times, myself.

Personally, creating an Island of Sanity does not mean that all is sane within our organizations all the time; that is simply unrealistic. I have incorporated this approach into my work as a leader to include a profound respect for our organizations and those we serve. I have witnessed in the past decade significant tolls on my colleagues and students when the outside world is feeling anything but sane. All of what is going on outside of our organizations is out of our control, and our colleagues and clients know that, yet we have leadership positions and titles that connote command, control, and influence.

41

These points in time when our nation and the world are in great conflict are among the most difficult to make sense of or meaning out of. Even respectfully naming a conflict can be fraught with challenges. How can I convey my thoughts and emotions appropriately to be of support?

There have been countless times when all I could do was look for ways to influence my college community and sit and listen to my colleagues and students. Really listen. This was not easy at times as some colleagues have been in incredible pain, pain that is further provoked on the nightly news. Then, I would check in with impacted colleagues. Those check-ins, while important, always felt woefully insufficient when no words could ease their pain, grief, or fear.

Yes, leadership is, at times, lonely, and it does take a personal toll, especially after the pandemic years. Yet, we are still required to show up and realize that as much as we pride ourselves as pragmatic doers, sometimes the greatest challenge of leadership is listening to others with humility and empathy.

I see that effort by our Leaders as well in how they have led their respective communities, organizations, and businesses pre-pandemic, through the pandemic, and as we transition out of the emergency phase of the COVID-19 pandemic. Their professional foundations are strengthened by childhood independence, early leadership opportunities with exemplary mentors, and an uncanny sense of maneuvering around multiple professional obstacles. They were pivoting before *pivot* became a term that is now bemoaned as a pandemic descriptor that no one wants to hear any longer.

The Leaders were also working on systemic change methodically and from the inside without fanfare and without burning down their organizations altogether. Some Leaders have highlighted this Gen X trait as one that has served us well while working alongside Boomer bosses, mentors, and colleagues and now a trait that has left us questioning at times how to move forward as Millennial and Gen Z colleagues are calling for immediate change. We are the bridge to the future, yet how do we ensure that bridge is firmly in place? I keep returning to those aspirational Islands of Sanity, one by one, connected by the Gen X bridge builders.

Leading While at Midlife

What inspires me the most is that the Leaders have survived and thrived during immense leadership challenges during and after pandemic *and* our nation's Racial Reckoning, all while managing immense personal pressures that inevitably come with midlife. Once again, I am compelled to liken midlife as comparable to being in the hot middle of the panini press, squeezed from both sides. We are caring for children (many of whom are teenagers;

need I say more?), caring for aging parents, dealing with economic uncertainty, navigating tremendous changes at our workplaces, managing our own health challenges emerging at midlife, and then adding a once-in-100-year pandemic on top of this—that's a lot of pressure upon one of the smallest generational cohorts.

We also know that as we come out of the COVID-19 pandemic, grief and loss underscore this time like never before. I rarely speak to a fellow Gen Xer who hasn't lost a parent or loved one these past few years. Even if they did not lose a loved one to COVID-19, they are caring for and/or responsible for loved ones for whom quality of life and care was certainly impacted by the crisis that COVID-19 has inflicted upon our nation's health care system.

Layer onto that grief and loss the impacts of long COVID, dramatic workplace changes, burnout, and the loss of opportunity for our children and ourselves. How many fellow parents do we know who still grieve the loss that their high school or college seniors did not get to graduate or have a "normal" experience that we once took for granted? I know far too many parents have an alternative reel playing in their heads about how their children's lives would have evolved differently if the pandemic had not happened. At this point, as leaders, we should assume that everyone we work with or come in contact with has been impacted in some meaningful way by the COVID-19 pandemic. I am reminded of Dr. Warren Brown's sentiment that, as Gen X leaders, we need to be better about showing employees who we are. I couldn't agree more, even if it doesn't come naturally.

Some of the most meaningful conversations I've had with colleagues were after sharing that my father passed away at an all-college meeting (admittedly not the easiest news to share). I was so touched by their empathy. Some shared with me their own hair-graying struggles managing parental care and the ongoing grief they feel after losing a parent and/or a loved one. Once again, I am reminded that truly everyone is going through something.

Leadership Is Lonely and Takes a Toll

This section gets to the heart of why I wrote this book. I have been in so many one-on-one conversations with Gen Xers these past few years who led their organizations through incredible transitions and only quietly and privately shared the personal and professional toll that their leadership took. A significant amount of this toll was due to the stress of the pandemic, the 2020 Racial Reckoning, and the incredible pressure to make meaning and sense out of these extraordinary challenges. All while trying to ease the stress and uncertainty of those they are responsible for and fix all the organizational and personnel problems *immediately.* Leadership is a lonely job in the best of times, and that loneliness is certainly exacerbated during times of crisis.

Mayor Victoria Woodards shared a powerful and thoughtful insight to underscore these challenges as a leader during this time:

> Being a leader is tough. Even more so as a woman leader and a woman of color. Leadership is an even more difficult job to a black woman during a racial reckoning where I often felt that was not black enough (to some members of her community) and not white enough (for others). These last few years leading through such difficult times especially as a leader of color is very difficult to be in a position of having to preserve the institutions that she leads while also being harmed by those institutions.

I am so grateful that Mayor Victoria shared these thoughtful, albeit difficult-to-hear words. She has always been an inspirational leader and was especially so during such a challenging time as 2020. Despite feeling this incredible pressure, Mayor Victoria led Tacoma through a time of peaceful and respectful protest during the summer of 2020. "Tacoma did not burn," she said with determination and pride.

Dr. William Serrata describes the period from March 2020 to December 2021 as one in which "the concept of time was out the window and there was no concept of time zones either." That was particularly challenging while serving as the national chair for the American Association of Community Colleges and the Chair of Texas' fifty community colleges. He felt like he never stopped working, with weekly AACC meetings on top of running the college. William was the vice chair of the Texas community colleges during the time of George Floyd's was murder and our country's Racial Reckoning.

He stressed that "Texas is a red state, and the colleagues at all of the colleges could not agree on a statement to release together." So, William did what he felt was right for his El Paso community and publicized his statements. He received pushback from some faculty who were upset about statements while there were Racial Reckoning protests in El Paso. William tried to focus his sentiments and the college's resources to help with the healing of his student body, which is 85 percent Hispanic. "It was a troubled time which feels like a very long time ago."

Most of the Leaders I spoke with juggled health challenges throughout the pandemic. For William, he said it was an overwhelming time—he had his own challenge with a dental infection and a locked jaw for a couple of months. He lost thirty-five pounds, and while he could speak, he was unable to eat solid food for two months. Amazingly, he continued to work and lead during this time! In true Gen X sarcastic fashion, when I asked him how he got through this time, he replied with a half-smile, "I just did it and aged significantly."

The Art of the Pivot

Andrea Heuston shared a different determination, that of the *pivot*. She shared with me that her son graduated in the class of 2020, had a Zoom graduation, and got to walk across the stage at twenty-minute intervals. While that was challenging for her and her family, her son is happily working now. She is proud of her ability to manage her children's education during the pandemic shutdown while running a marketing and events management company. Yes, an *in-person* event management business in 2020.

Andrea's events business took a 50 percent hit in two months and was in the red for two years. After the start of the pandemic, she never went back to the office, although it took a while to get out of the lease. Her company survived with two Paycheck Protection Program (PPP) loans (that were eventually forgiven). Andrea said those loans helped to keep every person employed through the pandemic. She did so while moving out of town altogether due to health challenges that contributed to her being at significant risk had she been exposed to COVID-19. She spent most of the pandemic near the Pacific Ocean, managing her company and employees remotely. Andrea's story truly defines a pivot in the best sense of the word.

Feeling the Boomer Loss

Dr. Julie Pham admits that she has not felt the loss of the Boomers and their mass retirement as much in her day-to-day work life as the owner of CuriousityBased and author of *7 Forms of Respect*, as most of her colleagues are between the ages of twenty-six and forty-four. She notes that there are a lot of Gen Xers in tech as well. That said, she has felt the impact in her personal life with the changing of her parents' generation and the stewardship of the Vietnamese community in Seattle. Julie said she had learned so much from her elders, and together, they shared their stressors and did the work. This transition "felt a bit scary and looked different . . . Gen X leaders don't speak Vietnamese because of the assimilation push and grew up in US . . . Plus, a lot of institutional memory was lost with newspaper leaders who were there since the 1990s."

For many of us across multiple sectors, the pandemic and ensuing Great Resignation certainly contributed to this sense that the institutional memory of our communities, organizations, and businesses retired along with the Boomers. I am not sure how to remedy that or its impact on our organizations other than to be mindful of the need to go beyond our usual succession planning and onboarding activities to make sure Millennials and Gen Z are not in this position when we retire. Ideally, we could set them up for success to not only understand why and how we operate organizationally but to then pick and choose intentionally what we want to carry forward together.

Gen X leaders are certainly more mindful of the scope of this loss of history and context as we worked most closely with the Boomers who led our businesses and organizations for decades. Certainly, Millennials are aware of the downstream effects. Also, I am very mindful of what a lack of succession planning looks like for Gen Z, who have their own full plate of issues that are top of mind for them. Many of us, therefore, feel a particularly acute responsibility to tie up as many loose ends as possible before handing off the leadership reigns to a Millennial or Gen Z successor.

Finally, I sense that Millennials already feel this transition, perhaps as much as we do with so much leadership churn. One anecdotal case in point: during the summer of 2022 my Boomer husband and I had brunch with his Millennial son who was telling me about how after four years his entire department turned over and he became the senior person in his division. He described how he had to make sure human resources was doing their job correctly so that his work was accurate. And then, out of the blue, he said something of a lightning bolt statement, "I really don't think there is any institutional memory anymore." I thought to myself, *This is not a Gen X leadership issue; this is a generational transition that is impacting us all.*

We Can't Wait for Perfection

Dr. Warren Brown is certainly no stranger to leading an organization during a crisis. As President of North Seattle College, he stewarded the college through a heartbreaking time when five international students were killed and over forty injured during a collision between their bus and one of Seattle's infamous Duck Boats.[2] This crash was devastating to the college community and, of course, the families impacted by the tragic loss of their adult children studying abroad.

As a peer colleague of Warren's at the time, I observed how he handled the national and local media intensity as the consummate professional I have always known him to be. I asked him, in preparation for this book, what lessons he took from that difficult time. He had a couple of important nuggets that I believe stand on their own:

- Don't let perfect be the enemy of good (one of my favorite sayings).
- There will always be criticism that you have not done enough.
- You can't assume you'll get 100 percent buy-in.
- Check yourself and act with integrity, not with fear.
- Recognize there are many agendas.

And there was one more important takeaway worth thinking about. Warren shared, "Don't believe the hype either . . . stay humble; stay transparent; [you are] never as good as your greatest supporter and never as bad as your worst critic." We should all reread this section on our toughest days, reflecting on letting go of the unrealistic expectations surrounding leadership today and moving forward to the best of our abilities, especially during this time of tremendous challenge and transition.

Warren's leadership challenges continued upon leaving the community and technical college system as he transitioned to leading a philanthropic organization focused on student support. Warren described the organization he was hired to lead in 2020 as an organization where the foundation CEO was a Boomer, the board was mostly Boomers, and the organization was very structured and all about "the rules." When George Floyd was murdered in the summer of 2020 and the Racial Reckoning was underway, Warren knew it was time to take another look at the organization's mission, which was focused on access, and begin to focus in earnest on equity.

Warren experienced pushback from some board members who were resistant to changing the mission to incorporate DEI versus solely focusing on access. Warren knew, however, that he couldn't wait for everyone to agree as he knew there would not be consensus. "Social justice can't wait to get everyone on board." Warren discussed the need to get to majority rule as opposed to consensus with his board and then move forward while staying within his integrity. No small feat given that he was a new executive director during a pandemic, with children of his own, trying to make systemic changes.

Tales from the Bunker: My Story of Gen X Crisis Leadership

I will never forget the day that I found out that COVID-19 had come to my community. It had been a busy but surprisingly sunny and cheerful winter weekend (correct, it doesn't rain *every* day in Seattle). My mom had come over to spend some time with my son and me. We had lunch. Of course, it was Saturday, February 29, 2020. Leap Day. I woke up excited for this day reflecting about how amazing it was that it was Leap Day in the year 2020 and how much potential this year had in store for all of us.

Of course, I was aware of COVID-19. In fact, the week before I had seen the local hospital CEO and our mayor at a local breakfast and asked them about whether we *should* have a conversation about what happens if COVID-19 comes to our town. I had a conversation with my executive team about having a tabletop exercise with the City of Kirkland, which we scheduled with the city's emergency manager on March 10, 2020 (we later had an awkward laugh about that tabletop exercise while in the Emergency

Operations Center (EOC) on March 10). I had a conversation with my colleagues and all the presidents on Friday, February 28, the day prior, as we all sat in a room (one with minimal ventilation), seated closely together talking about what might happen if COVID-19 comes to Washington State.

Little did we know that COVID-19 was already here, spreading and unfortunately taking the lives of those rehabilitating at the Life Care Center of Kirkland. Yes, later that fateful Saturday, I would find out news about our exposed students that would force us to take a substantial leap into some seriously unchartered territory.

On the afternoon of Leap Day 2020, my vice-president for instruction called me to tell me that a group of eighteen first-quarter nursing students had been exposed to COVID-19 while engaged with hands-on instruction at Life Care Center of Kirkland. A few of our faculty were exposed as well. My mind raced, and I had a growing pit in my stomach. I knew instinctively that life as we knew it was going to be very different going forward. I couldn't articulate at the time what that meant, but I knew something was very wrong. While my community had the dubious distinction of being ground zero for the US COVID-19 pandemic outbreak, my college had an equally dubious distinction of being referred to as "Campus Zero" by *The Chronicle of Higher Education*.[3]

What happened shortly thereafter is quite honestly a blur. I knew that our campus was in a full-blown emergency, and we had few details and no guidance as to what to do next to support our exposed students and faculty. While we closed for a few days to disinfect our college (little did we know that COVID-19 was airborne), the afternoon of our first day back, I received a call from public health that one of our exposed faculty tested positive for COVID-19. When I asked what I was supposed to do with that information, I was told I would get a call back from the CDC with next steps. To this day, over four years later, the CDC has never called me back (clearly and respectfully, they were busy). At that point, I knew no one had a handle on this outbreak, and we needed to close the college until we had more answers.

I am eternally grateful to the City of Kirkland for opening its Emergency Operations Center (EOC) to me and my colleague Leslie Shattuck, our college's executive director for marketing and communications. Together, Leslie and I worked in a small windowless conference room that had one wall of cinder block; forever, it will be referred to as *The Bunker*. For nearly three weeks in the EOC, we responded to over 160 media calls, communicated at least once a day with the college community, and held multi-hour executive team calls that resulted in triaging everything from student health to moving technical college classes online to massive purchases of laptops, etc. We knew what the rest of the country did not want to admit yet . . . this was going to be very scary, would take a while to get through, and we needed to prepare *now*.

Some days, I still don't know how my colleagues or I got through that period. I will tell you that my Boomer husband was a godsend, and my son was a young adult and self-sufficient. They took good care of each other and me while I was in The Bunker. The college had incredible support from our board of trustees, the city, and the state board for community and technical colleges. The congresswoman came by, city leadership came by (then we were all unmasked, of course), and the news media, while intense to work with, tried to help us get answers to our questions. How do I help our exposed students? How long do they have to stay at home? What are the COVID-19 symptoms anyway?

I had an amazing executive team whom I refer to as the Dream Team (still do, although one is now the president of her own college). I also had a seven-year-long foundation of a relationship with my college community. There was mutual trust, and we got through. And while working every day in The Bunker, I was able to talk with Kirkland Fire leaders who also had exposed firefighters (who had been responding to Life Care Center as well). I learned a lot from them. They, too, were trying to figure out how to move forward; I was fortunate to work alongside them and then advise my staff and students accordingly.

In some ways, I agree with Dr. William Serrata that early 2020 seems like a long time ago and a very difficult time. In other ways, memories like flash-backs will pop up, and I remember every detail of that time, hopefully like none other that I will ever experience again. Today, you can still see every piece of correspondence I sent out during the early days of the pandemic, media coverage, etc. I tend not to dwell on that time, and I've never gone back to watch myself on television. Instead, I focus my energy on the future. Much like William, I, too, had a subsequent year of dental work after far too much clenching and grinding of teeth.

One of the most surprising and meta-aspects of this period was that a doctoral student from my alma mater, the University of Nebraska-Lincoln, wrote her doctoral dissertation about our experience as Campus Zero. Talk about a surreal experience, reading a research paper that tried to explain and put an academic framework around a time in your life that was without explanation.

GEN X LEADERSHIP REFLECTION QUESTIONS

1. How do you describe your Gen X childhood? Can you see some aspects of your childhood in the Leaders' stories? This may be an opportunity

to reflect upon how your childhood and early professional opportunities laid a foundation for where you are today.

2. With the Boomer mentorship reflections, are there mentors in your life whom you could thank for their support along the way in your professional journey?

3. Were there Boomers who perhaps knowingly or unknowingly created professional obstacles for you?

4. Who are you mentoring formally or informally? Do you have time to support them as you would like to have been supported, guided, or coached?

5. What are the components of your own *midlife panini press*? How are you handling those components right now? Are there ways to lighten your load and/or recognize that you will not be in this phase forever?

ACTION STEPS: INCORPORATE LESSONS FROM GEN X LEADERSHIP

Reflect with gratitude Boomer mentorship and support. Remember all they did to raise you and support you professionally and personally. Try to keep those ties in place, even if periodically. When I made it to twenty years in the system, I wrote thank you notes to twenty individuals who impacted my career. I was inspired by *The Thank-You Project* by Nancy Davis-Kho.[4]

Recognize that while leadership feels lonely, you are not alone. The toll of leadership during the past four years and in the years ahead is real, professionally and personally. The people who know you and matter most to you know your work and know what you have accomplished. While you may or may not have received an award for this work, take stock that you are the go-to, reliable leader Millennials and Gen Z are looking for. These Leader stories are just a few examples of the toll of leadership and how you are not alone.

Begin to rebuild your board of directors and safety net. Keep trying to knit your professional and personal safety net back together. Now is a good time to take stock of your mentors, health care providers, friends, and family. All indications are that longevity and health span come down to strong social ties and community. With the Great Resignation, many aspects of that professional community have been impacted. More on that in part III.

Source: Getty Images, XiaoYun Li

PART III

The Path Forward: Six Steps to Sustain Ourselves and Our Organizations While in the Middle of the Panini Press of Life

Chapter Ten

Step One

Creating the Organizations We Wanted at the Beginning of Our Careers

Before I begin this final section and offer some support to my fellow Gen Xers, I want to name the fact that we are in midlife and in the middle of life—in the hot, challenging, and smack-dab-middle of what I refer to as the *panini press of life*.

As a working mother of a hungry son, I love my panini press. It was a fiftieth birthday gift from my mother—what could be better and more symbolic? While I am waiting for the grilled cheese sandwiches to finish, I often think about how we, as Gen Xers, parents, and leaders, have pressure from both sides of the great panini press of life—caring for our children, our organizations, and our parents and elders.

In December, as I try to squeeze in time to write a few chapters in this book, I turned fifty, and my Dad, a veteran who, after a decade-plus of fighting Parkinson's disease, passed away. I share that with you to say that by the time we all get to this point in life, we all have some proverbial grill marks, and we'll be a little crispy around the edges. But just like that perfect panini, we are something to appreciate. Most of all, we should take some time to appreciate who we are and how far we have come while in the crucible of life.

It is in that spirit of recognizing and naming what we have been through and what we have to offer that this first chapter of part III is framed. I hope this chapter provides you with pragmatic, hopeful, and comforting guidance as you move forward—as much as a perfect grilled cheese panini and bowl of hot tomato soup, made with a mother's love of course, can provide on a cold and rainy Seattle day.

One of the more challenging times in my career was in my mid-thirties balancing work and motherhood. My son was a toddler, and his father and I had full-time careers. While we were incredibly fortunate to have doting grandmothers nearby, I was still juggling work five days a week, trying to have some flexibility to spend time with my son and begin work on my doctorate. Then, it was a herculean task to request one day a week to work at home. I was granted one telecommute day in a circuitous way (my outgoing boss put a letter of permission in my human resources file for the incoming boss), and lo and behold every telework day, my boss would call me. I panicked if my son was making any noise at all. I thought for sure I would lose that precious benefit and that precious time with him. It was a very stressful time for certain.

It was at that point that decided I wanted to lead a college community that understood and valued working parents and all that we juggle. To this day, one of the most joyful parts of my job is seeing my colleagues' children grow and thrive through the years. I welcome their children with gusto to every campus event that they can attend and thank their parents for bringing them to campus. During our years of pandemic all-college virtual meetings, we'd start some of the meetings with a pet and baby/kid cam, when all the kiddos and fur babies could show their faces on camera. It brought much-needed delight to all of us. One employee told me recently how much she appreciated how supportive the college was to her as a working parent. She had no idea how grateful I was to hear that comment and how hard we all worked to create that culture.

As we come out of the pandemic emergency phase, as leaders, we have an opportunity to reflect on our own challenges around balancing our lives against the "five-days-a-week, I-need-to-see-the-whites-of your-eyes" primarily Boomer work ethic with which we were raised professionally. Heck, I think after the pandemic, most Boomers don't want to work the way they once did either, which is why many retired.

At this point, I am aware that many employees and leaders cannot work in a remote or flexible way. To all the essential workers who took care of us, our children, our parents, and those who kept us safe during the pandemic, I want to convey my sincere gratitude. I saw first-hand the toll that the pandemic especially took on our health care workforce near the end of the pandemic as my dad was in and out of the hospital, rehab, and assisted living. I know from friends and family the toll the pandemic has had on our first responders as well. They are true heroes.

SELF-CARE IS OUR JOB

As leaders, we strive to care for and curb the burnout of our employees, no matter the industry. There is an opportunity before us to find that sweet spot regarding how we work for our employees, colleagues, and ourselves. So, where is that sweet spot now for Gen X leaders? How can we best support our sanity while supporting our employees?

Within that sweet spot is a lot of complexity and room for personal and professional growth. One of the toughest and most important lessons I learned from a former Traditionalist boss was that no one was ever going to tell me to take a day off or take better care of myself. Maintaining my health and showing up every day with a healthy mindset is *my* job. No employee wants their leader showing up with their hair on fire, dark circles under their eyes, and a surly attitude (no matter how justified).

How many times as employees did our bosses show up to work in an upset state and we thought *we* did something wrong? I would never want my colleagues to think they were on the hot seat because, unbeknownst to them, I was having a bad morning. And yes, as leaders, we, too, have bad mornings, and yes, it is still our job to adjust our attitudes on our way to work. This is not easy, especially keeping ourselves calm and healthy with an adjusted mindset during the past three years. This is where we bring back Dr. Warren Brown's reminder not to let perfect be the enemy of good.

While I am not a wellness expert (although my pandemic "passion project" did include earning a holistic health coach certification), I have tried to incorporate and prioritize all aspects of better health for our community. This work for our community is an attempt to continue to support employees and students during the time when health—both physical and mental—must remain a top priority if we are going to lead our organization through to a successful future.

LEADING INCLUSIVE ORGANIZATIONS WITH HUMILITY

We all want healthy organizations, and if you are still reading this book, I would expect that you, too, want welcoming and inclusive organizations. The Leaders profiled in this book also talked about their hopes for inclusion and change in their organizations. Some shared the Gen X coming-of-age mindset that we would be the change we wanted to see in the world from the *inside* of those organizations, through policy and by incrementally making changes that lasted. That approach has been challenged these past couple of years as demands for immediate systemic change are made. As leaders, we need to respond, as well as be prepared, for the pushback and backlash like that of many of the Leaders faced when making changes to their organizations that were grounded in equity.

While I am by no means a DEI expert, I have tried earnestly to lead an institution that strives to be equitable, diverse, and inclusive and doing so with a heaping dose of humility and drive to learn more to do better, as inspired by the late Dr. Maya Angelou.[1] And still, by no means, have I got it all right. I have read, listened, reflected, and engaged with colleagues around uncomfortable conversations. Perhaps most importantly, I strive to support and create regular opportunities to learn and grow in community with my colleagues in a transparent and, at times, vulnerable way.

What has driven me is the end goal of creating an organization that is welcoming and inclusive of all our employees and students so that they can grow, achieve, and thrive in a physically and psychologically safe place. In 2016, our students created the RISE Center (Resources for Inclusion, Support, and Empowerment) inspired by a poem by Dr. Angelou.[2] Again, we are far from perfect and are always striving to do better by our students and colleagues.

I have been a keen observer these past few years as other employers have made sweeping public pronouncements about return to work only to retract or reframe those statements weeks later after employee pushback. Conversely, other organizations made announcements about everyone staying remote permanently. Like a true Gen Xer, I have tried to lead with the understanding that fundamentally, even within my college, every employee and their role is unique and demands its review in partnership with employees and their supervisor. For the most part, as the world begins to transition to its post-pandemic reality, that flexibility and willingness to adjust seem to resonate with employees. As one of my Millennial employees recently told me, "If you weren't as flexible as you are [as a boss], I would have left awhile back."

And isn't that what *we* wanted in the early parts of our careers? Inclusive organizations that recognize, welcome, and even celebrate our diversity? Bosses that understood that we have responsibilities outside of work and that we could still get the work done even if we weren't at our desks every day at 7:30 a.m.? Bosses that did not lead, as Dr. Warren Brown's did ("this is hard work"), but bosses that helped us when we needed it, got out of the way, and publicly gave us due credit for our work? As we build that bridge to the future can we safely assume that our Millennial and Gen Z colleagues would appreciate the same support?

ACTION STEPS: CREATE THE ORGANIZATIONS WE WANTED AT THE BEGINNING OF OUR CAREERS

Reflect on the organization you wanted to work in earlier in your career. What flexibility, support, and/or consideration did you want as a young employee that you did not receive from your Boomer boss? How can you offer that support to your current employees as well as to yourself? Can you ask your younger employees what they need now? Roundtables, office hours, management by walking around, and checking in via a short email, text, or even a phone call? Would those steps help inform how you continue to shape your organization going forward?

Ask your employees what you can help with. I know every organization has its own way of managing employee and customer feedback. Some of it is helpful, but other feedback seems perfunctory or, at worst, disingenuous. I try to end every employee meeting and most casual employee and student interactions with the questions "What can I help with?" or "How can I be helpful?" I also enlist other trusted members of the community—labor leaders and other committee chairs—to share anonymous feedback or follow-up questions with me. One colleague figured out how to receive anonymous questions and they answered them publicly.

How can you continue to develop as a leader in spaces where you are not an expert? Can you lean into areas where your employees need your support and learn from others? Two of my go-to resources for learning more about an area that I hear about from students or employees that I may not know enough about is searching for that topic on a podcast (I am not sure if there is any item that is not currently covered via a podcast) and/or LinkedIn Learning.

I have also learned during the pandemic that I may not always have time to sit and read a physical book or e-book, but I do have time and the capacity to listen to a podcast or audiobook while getting ready for the day, commuting, doing chores, etc. That has been one way I have been able to dive deep into certain subjects and keep pace with the current thinking and resources, especially around diversity, equity, and inclusion.

And of course, you can go old-school and ask your local librarian for recommended resources. A fun way to think about how to hold yourself accountable to personal growth is to check out Gretchen Rubin's Four Tendencies Quiz[3] and see what tendency you are (this is a fun team building exercise as well) and create accountability structures accordingly so you can lean into areas your organization needs and where you have not yet received formal training.

Chapter Eleven

Step Two

Nurturing a Community of Gen X Leaders

This chapter gets to another key reason why I wrote this book. After leading an organization through a once-in-a-lifetime global pandemic followed by a once-in-a-lifetime Racial Reckoning, followed by the retirement exodus of long-time Boomer colleagues, I realized that leadership can be isolating, and it can take a mental and physical toll. Due largely to the pandemic, the otherwise built-in physical opportunities for meeting with colleagues and fellow leaders at regular meetings, conferences, and other ad hoc gatherings were either canceled or relegated to an online format.

That format did not afford any meaningful conversations in the hallway while refilling my coffee during a break or walking toward another meeting. At a time when I needed to dig in with colleagues and check in on them, those opportunities and all of those important "weak ties"[1] evaporated for what seemed a long time. As the opportunity presented itself to have a phone or private virtual conversation, I knew I wasn't the only leader challenged with the overwhelming task of leading during extraordinary circumstances.

CREATING COMMUNITY WHEN YOU NEED IT MOST

I asked Dr. Warren Brown how he found a community that supported him during the Duck Boat crash crisis and then again as he transitioned to his non-profit role just ahead of the pandemic. Warren shared how he had already honed his network of working parents, CEOs, college presidents, high school, and personal friends. And he tried to expand and cultivate his network, "looking for those with different characteristics."

Warren is a consummate professional, and I appreciated that he called out how he openly expanded his network to "not just talk about policy and products but be open with colleagues." He advised, "Let your colleagues see you engage your children (for example) as you try to get them to see that you are a real person . . . model this balance." This is an important point that I have had to grapple with as a Gen Xer who does not have a Facebook account. Warren and a few other Leaders noted how our default toward privacy is contrasted with the seemingly over-sharing of Millennials and Gen Z. Honestly, sharing some of the few personal and professional details in this book is a stretch for me; my default tendency is to keep my social media presence focused solely on work.

Warren contrasted his approach of striving to be more open with the example set by his Boomer father. He shared that when his Boomer father passed, very few colleagues knew about this personal life and vice versa. He worked at City Light for many years, and went to drinks with colleagues but did not disclose personal information about family, and so on. I think this guardedness and weighting of privacy is part of our Gen X professional upbringing, taught to us by Boomers. This approach is certainly one that we continue to work through as we strive to strengthen our multi-generational networks.

And yet, our networks of Gen X leaders are a vital part of our endurance in this bridge-building exercise. I received wise counsel during the pandemic to work to widen my lens, or *aperture*, on how I am viewing my work by expanding my network. I took this work seriously and engaged in the following exercises:

- Sent notes to those whose work I appreciated and admired via LinkedIn.
- Emailed professional "loose ties" to have a quick Zoom session and see how they were doing.
- Participated in virtual conferences and sent any connections a quick note to check in on them and compare notes about the conference.
- Organized regular check-ins with colleagues also managing work and children learning at home.
- Created my own "mastermind" groups with women presidents to work through campus issues (more on this later).

The result? A stronger network of Gen X and other leaders to whom I remain connected even today. A network of leaders whom I feel like I can call upon when I need advice, inspiration, empathy, and to brainstorm what's next. That, coupled with the restoration of in-person regular meetings, conferences, and gatherings, has helped to afford me the opportunity to regularly check in with colleagues and try to keep the finger on the pulse of our college communities.

Warren also made an important point when it comes to creating community: "Our Gen X retirements will not look like traditional Boomer retirements." You only need to look at the soaring rates of new entrepreneurial efforts and businesses launched by those in midlife[2] to see that Gen Xers will be working for a very long time for a variety of reasons. We have all seen the number of Boomers who have "unretired" and returned to work in some capacity. We have gleaned from their experiences that retirement is much more nuanced than we originally thought. A robust, multigenerational network is a key component to not only employment opportunities, but the satisfaction that comes with an engaging colleague and friend with whom you can share your journey, and if you are fortunate, with whom you can let go some of your stressors.

Naming Our Worries at Midlife: The Empty Nest

Speaking of worries, midlife is chock full of worries, and worrying may be considered by some as a midlife hobby. Worrying about school safety, online safety, exposure to COVID, long COVID, eldercare, relationships, friendships, the economy, wars abroad, cyber security, the next election . . . shall I continue? There is something surreal about midlife when your child(ren) "leaves the nest," and you lose your parents as well.

There is something about the Gen X parent dynamic, at least anecdotally, where we were as proportionately over-involved in our children's lives as our parents were proportionately laissez-faire about ours. This sentiment is underscored in *Generations*, where Twenge attempts to underscore the angst that Gen X parents feel about raising our Gen Z children.

> Even as they glorify their independent childhoods, many Gen Xers are also now the parents who protect—and sometimes overprotect—their kids . . . Other Gen X parents would love for their children to put down their smartphones and get out of the house, but have given up trying to fight Gen Z's technology obsession. Still, many Gen Xers want to make sure their kids don't do the same dumb stuff they did, looking back on their childhoods with a combination of nostalgia and postponed terror: How they wonder, did they manage to make it out alive? (p. 165).[3]

This quote sums up so perfectly the tensions of Gen X parents of our Gen Z children and all that they are facing in the world today, challenges that we could not have even imagined or wanted to imagine growing up.

My son will soon be leaving for college. Many well-meaning friends and colleagues ask me how I am doing with the prospect of my son leaving for college. Am I happy? Sad? Will I cry? Honestly, yes to all. It is a bittersweet time of life. Many of us juggled family responsibilities with raising children for decades, and then that phase of life is suddenly over. Heck, I wore the working mother title as a badge of honor.

And yet, I know that while my son will no longer be under my roof full-time, his college departure is far different from my own. He won't call me only on Sundays, and he's not moving multiple states away to only come home for the holidays (one holiday, I didn't even come home). Chances are, I will continue to be in regular contact, and chances are he'll continue to call me in the middle of meetings, just as he has since he first got a cell phone in middle school.

Naming Our Worries at Midlife: Caring for Our Aging Parents

The bottom line for Gen Xers is that the empty nest is not without great additional responsibility. Indeed, no one can prepare you for parenting, and we can all agree with teenagers and young adults that this is true. And our society does not prepare us to manage the care of our parents either. When my father was sick with Parkinson's (a particularly cruel disease), I had some of the most meaningful conversations with friends and colleagues about caring for a parent and how overwhelming it can be.

The toll of caregiving is undoubtedly felt acutely by those of us at midlife as we care for our parents as well as our children. Yes, we are smack in the middle of the "Sandwich Generation." At this point, I want to implore us as leaders to expand our understanding of the caregiving crisis, one that is dramatically impacting not only those of us at midlife, but also our younger Millennial colleagues. This is not just a Gen X dynamic. An eye-opening episode from *The Sunday Read*, a special edition of the *New York Times* podcast, *The Daily*, called "The Agony of Putting Your Life on Hold to Care for Your Parents," speaks to the impact that caregiving has on Millennials who are trying to grow their careers while caring for their parents and younger children as well. This extended span of caregiving[4] is certainly a dynamic I have seen in my workplace as younger, mostly female, colleagues have relocated or stepped away from their jobs to care for parents.

As leaders, the pressures of caregiving while in the middle of the sandwich generation can be overwhelming. We are facing substantial challenges personally while managing the care of our children and our parents. We walk into meetings, speeches, and presentations, holding our breath and hoping we don't get a call in the middle of our presentation, that we have to take, to get a critical update from our parents' caregivers. As leaders, we are also mindful of the support our colleagues need to care for their sick children, parents in the hospital, or critical medical appointments, all of which happen during *our collective* workday.

If, as leaders, we have some flexibility within our workday, we can technically manage these challenges. However, we are also mindful of the example that we are setting for our colleagues. The bottom line is that caregiving has a dramatic impact on our emotional, mental, and physical health. That impact is compounded by our expectations of ourselves as leaders and that of our employees and clients. No one is perfect at this phase of life. Again, I implore you, during this most vulnerable of times, to be as kind and supportive to yourself as you would be to your best friend or your employee.

Taking Time with Our Community for Our Long-Term Health

Finally, let's circle back to Warren's earlier point that "our retirement will not look like traditional Boomer retirements." One dynamic that always befuddled me was when a Boomer retired, they seemed to transition to another realm, one in which our paths rarely crossed again. I was always amazed by that dynamic. Especially colleagues with whom I worked closely. Maybe they wanted it that way? Maybe we had little in common after they left work? Maybe that is the societal norm? Perhaps there can be a new norm where work friends remain friendly after you leave or they retire. If appropriate, perhaps those important work friendships can follow you into your next job, next business, and/or your next chapter. Given that CNN proclaims that social isolation is deadly, perhaps we should all redouble our efforts to expand our friendship networks as broadly as possible.[5] The bottom line: if we are all going to get pretty close to *The 100-Year Life* as proclaimed by Lynda Gratton,[6] a wide and robust network of Gen X as well as Boomers, Millennials, and Gen Z colleagues are not only ideal, but necessary.

ACTION STEPS: NURTURE A COMMUNITY OF GEN X LEADERS

Expand your network as wide as you can. Think about Warren's advice about going beyond your professional and personal networks to those who are different than you, with different paths, interests, and lived experiences. Can you look for opportunities to expand your network? If you would like more ways to expand your network, there are some great concrete and pragmatic steps in time management expert Laura Vanderkam's *Tranquility by Tuesday.*[7]

Form your mastermind group. There is nothing special about a mastermind group. They are not only for Silicon Valley investors. I think of many mastermind groups in which those who have common interests and goals can support each other and serve as accountability partners. These groups are particularly robust in the entrepreneurial space. Are there others that you could consider joining? Could you form your own? I originally knew two of the four women who make up one of my groups, and one of the women leaders invited the fourth. After meeting for the past couple of years, we are equally committed to each other's personal and professional growth and success. This has been an invaluable group with whom I can talk about several issues that impact women leaders.

Find empathetic leaders. I cannot stress enough how critical it is to have trusted colleagues who surround you every day. I refer to my direct reports as "The Dream Team" because of their expertise, support of one another, and how well we work together. We are not perfect, but truly, I look forward to going to work every day and working alongside my colleagues some ten years on.

Consider this network a critical component of your personal and professional longevity and sustainability. One of the more influential books we should all read is *The 100-Year Life* by Lynda Gratton. She wrote an incredibly thought-provoking work about how we can think about family, careers, entrepreneurism, and health span within the framework of living to 100 (should we be so fortunate to do so). One of my most significant takeaways after reading the book a few years ago is the importance of friendships and connections from a variety of ages, as well as the importance of thinking through the various stages of one's life and planning as if one will make it to 100.

Prepare yourself for the empty nest and the continuum of adult caregiving: This action step comes with the utmost care and advice. Most likely, by now, you have served in a caregiving role, and you know how demanding it can be, especially as you juggle a demanding career and other personal demands that could include raising children and caring for family or other loved ones. It's important to acknowledge this is a very bittersweet phase of life that often includes milestone celebrations, as well as celebrations of life, all within the same year. If you are a woman reading this book, understand you are not alone. Again, I would check out the most recent The *New York Times* podcast *(The Daily's Sunday Read)*, "The Agony of Putting Your Life on Hold to Care for Your Parents,"[8] on the extended span of caregiving. And as difficult as this phase is, I ask that most of all, you be as kind as possible to yourself.

Chapter Twelve

Step Three

Staying Curious and Not Letting the Grind Grind Us Down

Gen X leadership has a marathon quality. We have been working for decades already, and many of us still have years to go before we truly retire. All the Leaders I spoke with talked about their own approaches to mindset and stress management while acknowledging that there is a grind and a toll to their roles, even if they are working in their "dream job." There has been so much change and disruption to our professional and personal lives, especially these past few years. When interviewing the Leaders, there is a shared mindset that is grounded in an approach to keep moving forward despite daunting obstacles.

The Leaders also acknowledged that our systems, colleagues, and organizations have fundamentally changed after the mass Boomer retirement exit. There are holes in the organizational dam that we will need to plug ourselves, even if no one else knows they are there. There are gaps left behind by the Boomer exodus that only we will see. We will need to be the ones to call out those gaps, talk about how to fill them, and then lead to make sure they are addressed, and do so while onboarding new employees in demanding roles left open by retiring Boomers. No one else is going to do this work. Remember the unofficial Gen X theme song by Marlo Thomas, "Free to Be You and Me"? Filling the institutional memory gap left by the Boomer exodus while building a bridge to the future, well, that is up to us.

That pressure of making sure our organizations are stable and moving forward after so much disruption compounds the already serious grind to leadership that few see—hiring, firing, coaching, repeat. Active listening, guiding to the next phase, waiting for the next shoe to drop, managing public relations, managing up and down the organizational ladder, and providing peer support. We know change is constant, and everyone is tired of the pandemic pivoting. Still, our job as leaders is to keep our mindset healthy and to show up every day prepared for what is ahead of us, even if we are struggling personally. The leadership component of keeping pace with the grind of management while keeping one's mindset as healthy as possible is among one of the most challenging responsibilities of leadership.

Compounding this toll of leadership is knowing that if we are going to build trust and lead with integrity, we are going to have to stay open to others and to our inner voice and continue to learn, guide, and coach. Openness is the path forward, as difficult as it is. The critical component of this openness is approaching each day with curiosity, not ego. This, of course, is much harder than it sounds. I have a few thoughts to share from our Leaders and a few thoughts of my own as to how I have stayed open and curious these past few years and tried to not, in the words of my late and beloved grandmother, "let the turkeys get you down."

"It's a New Day Every Day"

When I think about the Leaders who faced leadership challenges while under the glaring spotlight of the pandemic, I think of Mayor Victoria Woodards and President William Serrata. Their willingness to stay open to the needs of their respective constituencies while facing public criticism and personal challenges is laudable. Mayor Victoria talked openly about how she feels "very responsible" for her employees and community. Almost to a fault, she said. "That attitude," she says, "costs something."

The mayor added that she feels Boomers and Gen X "sacrifice themselves" for their work. Like many Gen X leaders I know, and those interviewed in this book, the mayor's health was challenged during the stressful response of the last few years. She said her phone is always on . . . and that while "I am trying to take care of myself, that continues to be challenge." The mayor shared a gem of a piece of advice for Gen X leaders,

> Now more than ever, we have to walk confidently in our experiences without necessarily becoming Boomers. It's important, the idea of being authentic and telling the truth by being vulnerable, not comfortable. I don't have all the answers, but I find the best solutions and put a lot of pressure on myself and others, and if it doesn't work, we try something else, including failing forward. Progress, not perfection.

Mayor Victoria also stressed that while we have learned a lot from our Boomer mentors and leaders, "we need to learn from Gen Z and Millennials and sustain ourselves." One of the ways in which she sustains herself is through humor and laughter and "not just taking myself and others too seriously."

Some may accuse Victoria of being too "Pollyanna-ish." She said, "I have to keep optimistic because if I don't, I'll lose it. Even with optimism we need to have hope." She continues that if she carried all the weight of her role all of the time, she would never get out of bed. "It's a new day every day. Every day there's an opportunity to feed the soul. Every day there's an opportunity to continue forward." Her challenge to herself is that she still needs to learn to rest and take time. "Once in a while it helps to be silly!" Honestly, I think this approach takes incredible courage. Humor, optimism, and action can be a powerful antidote to the grind of leadership.

Take the Time to Take Care of Yourself

Dr. William Serrata, chair of the Texas State Community College Association, said that he started to look through the list serve of Texas community college presidents and realized that thirty-seven out of fifty had retired or exited by 2022 (I engaged in a similar daunting exercise). By the end of 2023, just eleven presidents remained with more seniority than Dr. Serrata. William found himself in an unexpectedly sudden role of senior president with a governing board of trustees where only a few of the trustees who hired him were left on the board. He described this entire accounting of collegial transition as "unnerving." I can empathize.

Through these significant leadership transitions, William said, "we've focused on continuing to serve students and focus on them, their safety, and security." However, he knows the past couple of years have taken a toll on him, and while these last few years there was certainly no shortage of work to do, "I wish I had taken more time off to deal with health issues. Leaders have to be healthy to take care of others."

"Ageism Is Real"

While many of us are still working through our leadership path forward, Dr. Julie Pham helped put the leadership grind in perspective, "We can't work any longer with the tendency that information is a need-to-know basis, that just doesn't work anymore . . . we need to be more transparent and people will help you if you need help." She recognizes one of the struggles of our generation as leaders and otherwise that "Gen X pushes against TMI . . . but that transparency can be useful."

Julie also shared an important and hard-to-hear piece of advice for Gen X leaders. "At some point all of us will feel obsolete . . . there will always be younger, more talented people. It's better to help them when you can, you want them to help you when they come up and catch up." This sage advice is underscored by the fact that our generation is one of the smaller age cohorts with Millennials and Gen Z working right along with us. I am sure many Gen Xers have asked themselves whether the Millennials have already passed us by. Julie drives home the point, "Ageism is real. It happened to Boomers and it will happen to us." She encourages all of us to consider what is our next act before it happens to us.

Building on Your Strengths to Cultivate Your Curiosity

One of the great gifts of writing this book was the opportunity to spend a concentrated block of time with the Leaders. Knowing them in different ways for varying amounts of time and then asking them questions about their childhoods, professional trajectories, and how they have led through these past few years has provided me inspiration, validation, reassurance, and a great deal of hope for the future. It also highlighted for me that we are all working in areas where we want to be, doing work that, for the most part, is what we have strived for and prepared for many years, if not decades, at this point. And still, leadership currently, and especially during the pandemic, has taken a substantial toll on our health and upon our organizations. Some Leaders left that work and created their own organizations, others sought different roles, and still others stayed in their current roles and continued to move forward while evaluating how to sustain themselves for the remainder of their careers.

The crisis response mode of the pandemic years was one that our Leaders stepped up to and met the moment. The pandemic essentially obliterated the ability for leaders to get a wider perspective. Who had the time or ability to turn their cell phone off and step away from the crisis response mode? The pervasive expectation of always being on has accelerated the burnout that we are seeing across the workforce. As leaders, one of the most difficult dynamics of the past few years is being able to step away and recharge. My heart sank when William said he was looking forward to a long-postponed vacation with his family in 2022, and then COVID had other plans. And yet, it is our job as leaders to make sure we are not burned out and can see our organizations through while proactively maintaining our health.

Like many of you, I have worked regularly on my mindset. I have read many of the leadership books one would find in an airport bookstore, retooled my morning routine (multiple times), meditated, journaled, exercised, got up at 5 o'clock (some mornings before so), and even worked diligently to "eat the frog." All this continual learning was in pursuit of showing up to work ready, rested, grounded, and prepared as a leader. Clearly, the pandemic upended many of those well-intended plans, and yet many habits have prevailed. For me, focusing on sleep and feeding my unending curiosity have been two tools that have helped me move through the past few years.

Not surprisingly, one of my Strengths Finder[1] strengths is that of Learner. Therefore, it's no surprise I work in higher education. I am always looking for what to read next, listen to next, and which podcasts to download. My curated podcast collection is at seventy shows and climbing, plus Audible, Kindle, and the ever-growing stack of books on my desk and nightstand. If you are an auditory learner or processor, you may consider taking a deep dive into podcasts. There is an incredible range of topics, experts, and opinions that can help you process and think through your approach to leadership for the long term. Plus, you can listen while driving, exercising, doing chores, and/or multitasking. One earbud in, and you are ready to take a deep dive into an area that befuddles you, that you need to learn more about, and/or think through.

ACTION STEPS: STAY CURIOUS AND DON'T LET THE GRIND GRIND US DOWN

"It's a new day every day." Humor and optimism can be part of a toolkit that provides an antidote to the grind of leadership. How are you keeping optimistic, incorporating laughter, and even being silly? Are you laughing enough? Are you hopeful for your future and that of your organization? If not, how can you reorient to provide more opportunities for fun? Laura Vanderkam's *Tranquility by Tuesday* mentions doing something for yourself one day each week.[2] Is there such an opportunity for you to step away? Especially now that the kids are possibly older and out of the house, can you even incorporate humor into your life?

Take care of yourself. How well or not are you doing physically and mentally? Gen Xers have long been told to suck it up and keep going. Yet, we do not treat others accordingly. Do you give yourself the same grace and encouragement that you give your younger colleagues? If you encourage your employees to take mental health days, be proactive as health issues come up, and seek counseling as needed. Do you afford yourself the same capacity? If not, why not? I encourage you to ask yourself, "How would I treat my employee in this case? Am I treating myself at least as well as I would treat my employees?"

Ageism is real. I love that Dr. Julie Pham called this out. This is a particular Gen X dynamic that when we came of age professionally, we were surrounded by Boomers, and we were always the youngest in the room. There was never a time when we were surrounded solely by Gen Xers. Then, seemingly one day, Millennials entered *en masse*, and now our children's generation is entering the workforce. Some days, we ask, *How did this happen so quickly?* And yet, heeding Julie's advice, we should consider being mindful who we are helping on their way up, as we never know who we will need to call upon in our next act.

Foster endless curiosity. How are you updating and revitalizing your daily routines and inputs? Are you proactively starting each day with time to yourself, or do you feel like each day is a sprint and you wake up behind? I've done both, and that's okay. I invite you to make time for reading, listening, tweaking your routines, and trying new things. Christine Koh's podcast, *Edit Your Life*, Hobbies episode,[3] notes that even when you are in the crucible of midlife, can you carve out time to feed your curiosity and create a bit of space in your life?

Chapter Thirteen

Step Four

Building the Bench While Calling the Shots

A question for you: do you remember where you were when you realized the Millennials had arrived? One day, I realized that the demographics of the workplace had fundamentally changed. It was a sunny summer day in Seattle around 2014 (always worth appreciating), and I was downtown for a rare midday errand when hundreds of very young people started walking in front of me. Clad with tech badges on lanyards, backpacks, wired earphones, and phones in hand (most looking down at them), a sea of humanity flowed out of Amazon headquarters into multiple destinations throughout downtown Seattle. I was a bit taken aback. Where did all these visibly very young adults come from? And where are they going? *The Millennials have arrived*, I thought. *And that means I am not the youngest in the workplace any longer.*

With this epiphany, I asked Millennials on my campus to meet with me to talk about their concerns, needs, and goals for the future as young colleagues. Many of them were working their way up through the ranks (many are directors, deans, and executive leaders today, and they are invaluable). In all the conversations we had that day, what stuck with me was what the term Millennial meant to them—the many sarcastic and frankly demeaning jokes that had been cracked at Millennials' expense had taken a toll. One employee even went so far as to say that there were so many negative Millennial stereotypes that they almost did not want to accept the meeting invitation (from me, the president) that had the word Millennial in the title. *Wow*, I thought, *popular culture really does a number on us*. I could empathize with being part of the "grunge generation" that was typecast as apathetic, lazy, and self-absorbed. So, let's first begin our bridge-building with our Millennial friends and colleagues by challenging our own biases that come with absorbing decades of generational stereotyping.

In fact, for most of us today, Millennials comprise our closest colleagues, trusted employees, perhaps even our bosses, and I hope some of our friends. We need to dispense with "the sky is falling" predictions that Millennials will take our leadership roles now that the Boomers have retired and that they will consume us by their sheer numbers. The bottom line is that we need our Millennial colleagues now more than ever, and they are critical to building our bridge to the future. They are, and will be, the keepers of institutional memory, and they will lead our organizations when(ever) we retire, if not before.

This chapter acknowledges our pop culture-hyped fears of a hostile Millennial takeover. It focuses on best practices from our Leaders about how to support and coach Millennials so that we are all more successful in the future. We can better prepare Millennial colleagues for current and future leadership roles, as we would have liked to have been mentored and supported. And yes, fellow jaded Gen Xer, we can learn a lot from the Millennials in many areas of work-life balance.

MOVING BEYOND RESENTMENT TO BEST PRACTICES

Dr. Julie Pham has created a multi-generational workplace as part of her company CuriosityBased. She notes that as a Gen Xer "I was okay with incremental change and buy-in," a different mindset than perhaps our younger colleagues. One of the tenants of her *7 Forms of Respect*[1] is that "just because you don't always get what you want doesn't mean that you aren't heard . . . be realistic. Change is hard." We can all take a page out of Julie's leadership handbook of channeling Gen X pragmatism when working with younger colleagues while focusing on how we can make sure Millennials are heard and respected in the workplace. Julie continues, "Gen X and Millennials need to get ahead of constant change and hang on to people." As leaders, we have felt this sentiment acutely during the past three years.

Compounding many leadership challenges is a very different set of expectations that Millennials and Gen Z have of the workplace. Millennial and Gen Z expectations for work-life balance far exceed the expectations that we began our careers with. As Warren reflected during his early career, Boomer onboarding included an expectation that either "we fit in or we don't fit." Julie and Andrea both touched on the importance of balancing Millennial and Gen Z personal and professional lives. Andrea observed from her employees that "Millennials typically last three years and then move on, some have come back though, which is gratifying," she notes, "they don't want 9 to 5 workplaces." Julie also notes that it is easy for Gen X to be resentful, "we should shape a workplace that we want to work for all of us."

Andrea Heuston offered many ways in which she, too, is creating a multigenerational workplace. First, Andrea wanted to point out that Gen X leaders were the true remote working trailblazers (with regular Boomer boss check-ins, of course). Since the pandemic, she has led a fully remote team with an overseas support team. Every day, she begins with an online team creative huddle.

Here are a few of her many rich nuggets of wisdom leading a multigenerational team:

- Honor the experiences of new people and try to incorporate them into the workplace culture as soon as possible.
- Connect Boomers and Millennial employees so that Boomers can learn from Millennials too—what some call reverse mentorship and the Danish refer to as *omvendt* or "turned around."
- Ask for suggestions and feedback regularly.
- Talk together across generations.
- Recognize excellence across the company (what her company Artitudes calls Star-titudes).
- Be open and truly listen to workers—let them be who they are as long as they get their work done—don't micromanage!
- Be open to new structures like part-time/flex-time.
- Figure out employee-centered approaches. Look to contractors for new ideas.
- Move money around to pay your employees competitively. If fast food is paying more than you are, you will need to pay more.

Today, Andrea's thriving workplace is made up of a few Boomers (remember her creative director emeritus designation? Genius!), a young Millennial, Gen Z, and Gen Xers, of course. She sees a lot of interest from younger employees who want to know what's next for them, and she works diligently to keep them supported and moving forward.

Preparing Millennials to Lead

Going back to the tension between Gen X work expectations that we had at the beginning of our careers compared to those of Millennials and Gen Z, Mayor Victoria added to that tension by raising some of the fear that comes with this transition. "Who is coming up behind us? Who will take our place, and what is their commitment?" While many Leaders talked about how our work ethic mirrors that of Boomers, Victoria noted that "Millennials and Gen Z do not have a Boomer work ethic and in many ways, I am envious." We should acknowledge outright that, yes, we are envious of that flexibility that is expected and demanded by our younger colleagues. At the same time, we were (very) lucky if we got to telework one day a week. We became leaders in part to carry forward what we learned from our Boomer bosses, and that's true, but we also became leaders to make our workplaces more flexible, especially for families like ours.

And so here we are with the most flexibility we have ever had in our careers and yet managing and leading those in a remote/flexible/hybrid environment is a challenge unto itself. Furthermore, we know we need to, as leaders, set our younger colleagues up for success with experiences, not just words. I appreciate what Mayor Victoria talked about during this part of our interview as she underscored that as Gen X leaders, we "need to be authentic and honest about expectations and what it takes to succeed even though that may be met with skepticism." She continued, "[we need to] put younger colleagues in positions to lead with experience as opposed to just talking about it and help leaders understand their why so that they could be put into places and feel and see the pressure that comes with it."

Like other Leaders, Mayor Victoria talked extensively about how integral her Boomer colleagues were in creating opportunities for her to step into leadership roles to gain critical experiences. That learning, side-by-side and through experience, is an important reminder of our work ahead. She emphasizes, "We simply cannot write off Millennials and Gen Z."

Trying to Do Right by Millennials

My hope for this chapter is not only to move beyond the Millennial stereotypes and discuss practical ways to support Millennial colleagues, but ultimately to do right by the next generations. I can clearly remember what it was like to try to manage a young child, a demanding career, and graduate school. At the time, I remember thinking that if I could only have one flexible day to work from home and focus on work and being present for my then-young son, I would be truly successful in balancing work and life. I was ultimately able to do so, but only with workplace resistance.

Gen X and Millennials are particularly impacted by the need for a work-life balance compounded by substantial disruptions to the care economy during the pandemic. Gen X and Millennial working parents were juggling work, educating their children at home, and increasingly caring for their parents. While I originally thought this to be a Gen X-Boomer squeeze, I was struck by a recent *New York Times* article that highlighted how impacted Millennials are by caring for their parents and family members as well.[2] This is an opportunity to support and lead younger colleagues who are just as squeezed as we are by caring for their children and parents at the same time. Pushing back against our Gen X tendencies not to share too much information, this is an opportunity to support our younger colleagues through workplace childcare, mental health support, and flexible work schedules and to share how we, too, are squeezed and trying to move through this pressure-filled time of life.

Investing in Leadership Development and Quality Childcare

Throughout my now decade of leadership as a college president at the same institution, there is a lot that I am proud of. I feel so fortunate every day to go to work and genuinely be glad to see whomever I am meeting with and run into in the hallways. By now, I know most of my colleagues well. I know their goals, about their children, their grandchildren, many of their burdens, and their joyful sources of pride. Albeit brief, these purposeful and ad hoc updates are among the most treasured parts of my day. And honestly, if I had not had seven years of those conversations and opportunities to cultivate work relationships under my belt, I am not sure I would have had the trust of the college to move us through the early hours of the pandemic.

With that said, there are two multigenerational best practices that I am proud of. One is our internal leadership development program, LEADS (Learning. Experiencing. Achieving. Developing. Succeeding.). In 2014, we recognized that we needed to not only recruit talented employees, but we also needed to retain our employees and grow our own leaders. In 2015, we launched the year-long internal development leadership program that focused on better understanding our college and our community and technical college system, as well as provided mentorship opportunities with our college's executive team.

A valuable part of the program has been the opportunity for LEADS members to work in small groups and tackle the challenges the college is facing. Then, at the end of the year, the leadership of the college listens to their thoughts about solving challenges ranging from internal communications to burnout. It has been so rewarding to see LEADS graduates develop their confidence throughout the year and then make impactful presentations at the end of the year. And, of course, it is especially rewarding when LEADS graduates are successfully promoted at the college. With five graduating cohorts, fifty-three of our employees have completed our internal LEADS program, and thirty-one employees are still at the college today. Of those thirty-one, nineteen have been promoted since they graduated from the program.

The other best practice is our sustained commitment to on-campus childcare. Certainly, if we learned anything during this pandemic, it is that childcare is essential. We have the good fortune of a childcare center on our campus, even though it is made up of twenty-five-year-old portables. This is why we are planning to build a new childcare center with federal, state, county, and local grant funds that became available during the pandemic. I cannot convey in words how critical safe, caring, accessible, and affordable childcare is to our students, our employees, and working families in our community. Our childcare workforce should be celebrated and appreciated for the essential workers that they are. At our campus, they were so courageous and were among the first employees to return to work in June 2020. I will never forget how hard they worked to continue to serve our students and community's children, no matter the ever-changing pandemic regulations and the risk to their own health and safety. Childcare workers are among the heroes of the pandemic.

ACTION STEPS: BUILD THE BENCH
WHILE CALLING THE SHOTS

Let go of outdated Millennial stereotypes. Millennials are forty now. They are adults with families and responsibilities, and with demands that are both similar and different to what we experienced when we were in our thirties and forties. It's time to update our meme-inspired thinking that Millennials are different and instead shift our thinking toward this generation as the recipient of our institutional memory and critical to our organization's enduring success.

Let's prepare Millennials for leadership roles when(ever) we retire. Dr. Julie Pham made another insightful comment that we should, as leaders, do all we can to help the younger generation up the career ladder because, ultimately, at some point, all of us will have a younger boss. Ageism is real, and we will need Millennials as we transition toward our next career and ultimately retirement.

Millennials as partners, colleagues, leaders, future leaders, and friends. What can we learn from Millennials? How can we advocate together for expanded childcare, elder care, and workplace flexibility? Can we grow our internal leadership development opportunities? Can we create opportunities for additional responsibility and leadership development? Bottom line: they need us, and we need them.

Chapter Fourteen

Step Five

Calling on Gen Z to Join Us and Be the Future We Need

This chapter may come across more as a love letter written with incredible empathy, hope, and love to the pandemic generation, often referred to as iGen, Zoomers, and/or Gen Z. I was reflecting the other day with another Gen Xer about where we were during the Challenger explosion, one of the defining historical moments of our generation. While that was a tragedy that resulted in the loss of life, impacted our global standing in the space race, and undoubtedly bruised our national ego, Gen Z's coming of age is marked by the COVID-19 global pandemic and all of its fallout.

As adults, we, too, are wrestling with the repercussions of the COVID-19 pandemic. Some of the most challenging times that I have had as a leader were making meaning of the events of the past three years and trying to provide reassurance to my community during the outbreak of the pandemic. Even finding the right words to use to describe the phase of the pandemic recovery we were in and trying to accurately describe how we were all feeling was very challenging some days. All while knowing full well that while I could empathize with how my community was feeling, I could not fully understand how diverse lived experiences intersected with all that the COVID-19 pandemic brought to light. Like many of our Leaders cited in this book, we all tried our best to remain humble, open, and empathetic to our constituencies and communities while trying to move forward.

While we have all struggled since the outbreak of the pandemic, I have a special place in my heart for the pandemic generation and their coming of age during COVID-19. It may take historians many years from now to fully make sense of all that we went through and all that we lost. Not unlike how historians today are still trying to understand how our nation dealt with the 1918 flu pandemic.

My son is a member of the Gen Z generation. He graduated high school in 2023. It's hard to convey how incredibly grateful I was that he was even able to physically graduate, in a large arena with our family present and without masks. Given that the graduating classes of 2020 and 2021 lost the opportunity to celebrate, gather with friends and family, and walk across the graduation stage, I felt incredibly grateful that graduation day. I sat during his graduation fully present with the love and gratitude in that arena for the hundreds of graduates that day who had endured so much, many of whom carried invisible scars from coming of age during the pandemic.

Professionally, I will forever be in awe that we are able to host in-person college graduations again after the pandemic. That I could shake our students' hands on stage, wish them well, and hand them their degree is a privilege I will never again take for granted. We have come so far since 2020, and yet so much work in our country and communities remains.

The COVID-19 pandemic shone a spotlight on so many of our country's inequities and glaring gaps that we need to close; perhaps first among them is the mental health toll the pandemic took on all of us, and especially Gen Z. I see it on my own campus that was fortunate enough to receive legislative funding for two full-time mental health counselors only for them to burn both out within their first year due to unending student needs. Jean Twenge attempts to capture the zeitgeist of Gen Z in her book, *Generations*, when she writes,

> This is Gen Z in a nutshell, concerned with authenticity, confronting free speech issues, pushing the norms of gender, and struggling with mental health . . . Gen Z is demanding our attention.[1]

Gen Z's mental health needs, and frankly that of all of ours, are not going to resolve themselves anytime soon. Can we model mental health in the workplace by supporting mental health access while getting the job done? How can we strike a balance as Gen X leaders who came of age during a time when no one talked about mental health or counseling at work or heck, even asked about how we were feeling most days? We came of age in a time when work and personal lives were separate, as Dr. Warren Brown discussed when reflecting upon his father's role modeling that he did not discuss family life at work.

Indeed, we are now in a very different time. Dr. Warren Brown encourages us to let our employees see more of ourselves, and Dr. Julie Pham invites us to push against our hesitancy to share too much. How can we adjust our TMI filters as leaders to better support younger generations who have very different expectations about workplace conversations and support? As I watch my own son come of age, I look to his early employment experiences and how his leadership has done an amazing job fostering growth through mentorship, regular professional development, on-the-spot coaching, and creating a fun atmosphere. Is there more we can learn from employers who primarily hire and rely upon younger workers?

When reflecting on how Gen X can build a bridge to the future, I think a great deal about how we can set Gen Z up for as much success as possible. I never understood the resignation and unreasonable expectations that came with the assumptions that the next generation is somehow going to possess superpowers we don't to fix all our current societal woes—especially racism and climate change. It's *all* our responsibility to cure what ails us for future generations.

How can we as leaders be empathetic while providing pragmatic coaching and management to set Gen Z up for success in the workforce? How can we guide young Gen Z employees so that they are prepared for a continued uncertain future? A future in which they can meet head-on, and yet they are not alone in fixing our many societal problems? Bottom line: with Gen Z, while we are in awe of their resilience, we're still going to need to do everything to help them change the world for the better.

ACTION STEPS: CALL ON OUR GEN Z CHILDREN, STUDENTS, AND COLLEAGUES TO JOIN US AND BE THE FUTURE

Management by coaching approach for Gen Z. As Gen X leaders who grew up alongside Boomer bosses and colleagues, watching and modeling their actions and behaviors, we need to be much more proactive and engaged with Gen Z. Management as coaching, highlighting wins, recognizing their contributions, helping them to set themselves up for future success. We can also engage them in reverse mentoring and allow them to show us what they can contribute.

Reconsider mental health in the workforce. I sincerely hope that after all we have gone through, Gen X leaders don't need to be convinced of the current importance of mental health access not only for employees, family, and ourselves. Can we, as leaders, talk openly about mental health and/or spotlight other leaders who do so? If you haven't already heard it, Congressman Adam Smith's interview with Andy Slavitt is worth a listen about how, as leaders, we can model vulnerability and talk openly about health challenges.[2] Can we as leaders advocate for access to mental health in our organizations through our employer-sponsored insurance plans and employee support efforts (EAP in Washington State)? Can we play a role in supporting the expanded pipeline of mental health providers? Can we, at the very least, work on our mental health to better support our employees, especially our Gen Z employees?

Gen Z is our future. Gen Z is emerging from the pandemic and finding their way. Instead of casting doubt or name-calling (I remember at the grocery check-out stand seeing *Time* magazine referring to us as the 'lazy, disaffected grunge rock generation' or the Millennials as the 'everyone gets a trophy' generation). Let's seek to understand this generation better and help them be as prepared and successful as possible. Are there examples in your community of non-profits, houses of worship, and/or employers who treat young people with care and respect, create a safe and fun work environment, and do a great job of providing on-the-spot coaching and mentoring?

Chapter Fifteen

Step Six

Calling in Our Boomer Retirees for Coaching, Mentoring, and Support

This book is concluding just as it began, impacted by the decisions and actions of our former Boomer mentors, bosses, colleagues, and clients. As Gen Xers, coming of age in the shadows of the Boomer generation, we always knew that at some point, our Boomer colleagues and friends would retire, and we would continue working. Heck, most of us came of age thinking that we would not only continue working past the Boomers but *long* past the Boomers, given the warning to our generation that we should not count on social security for our retirement due to projected insolvency.

In fairness, the Boomer retirement parade is not a surprise, however none of us could have predicted that the Boomers would seemingly retire at the same time, at the end of a global pandemic, leaving us to pick up the pieces. The fallout from this sudden demographic shift and our role in moving us toward a more multigenerational stable footing is the impetus for this book. And yet, Boomers, you're not off the hook just yet.

Andrea Heuston foresaw the Boomer retiree exodus. She saw clients retire, and when her key long-time creative director retired, she set into motion an employee emeritus program so that her creative director could stay engaged in the company and with colleagues. Andrea noted that for her, it was not only organizational knowledge and a strong work ethic that was lost with her Boomer retirements, but some of their "magic." She also noted that there was a feeling that her "safety net" was lost as well.

MENTALLY ADJUSTING TO OUR NEW PARADIGM (WITHOUT FULL-TIME BOOMER LEADERS)

Picking up on this feeling of a safety net and our (conscious or unconscious) association with the Boomers as integral parts of our own safety net. Boomers were there for us when we had questions, worries, crises. They provided reassurance, ideas, and solutions; they took care of problems and left us with an overall feeling that they had our back. I had this very conversation with my own team recently that we (an amazing team comprised of a soon-to-be-retiring Boomer, Cusp-er, mostly Gen Xers and a "geriatric" Millennial[1]) are on our own. We have the answers we need, but there is no senior go-to leader who will solve our problems; we are now the senior leaders that others come to for answers. We are our own safety net, and we need to create our own magic. This is a mental adjustment for all of us.

This transition is also an adjustment for many Boomers who retired during the pandemic or right afterward and are finding varying satisfaction from retirement. Many are looking for volunteer, part-time employment opportunities, and/or other ways to give back. How can we leverage this opportunity to provide what Andrea Heuston refers to as a "swinging door" for Boomers where they can come and go living their part-time work lifestyle? How can we create swinging doors in our organizations?

Finally, I want to make sure that Boomers and Gen Xers alike don't let each other slip away post-retirement. I think this is one of the most challenging and rarely-spoken-about aspects of retirement. We work with colleagues for many years, and then once they retire, we don't see them again. We all lose out on those touchpoints that we had when we worked together. Gen Xers, I know you have Boomer mentors who are both respected professional colleagues and friends. Those colleagues are important to your success and mental health. Those relationships are important for *both* of you going forward. How can you stay in touch? Have lunch or coffee regularly? Those relationships are not only critical to get us through this incredible period of transition post-pandemic but also for our own long-term vitality.

ACTION STEPS: CALL IN OUR BOOMER RETIREES FOR COACHING, MENTORING, AND SUPPORT

Create emeritus, consulting, and part-time opportunities for Boomer mentors. Are there opportunities in your organization for retirees to return to emeritus, part-time, adjunct, volunteer, and/or advisor work? Are there opportunities to look for "swinging doors" for Boomers that will support respecting their wishes to retire while honoring their intentions to still contribute while in retirement? Are retirees looking to you to discuss workforce reengagement? If so, take the call. We all want flexibility and we can learn and adapt from Baby Boomers' attempts at retirement to create our own retirement plan.

Rebuild your safety net. Now is the time for a mindset shift. There is no one else who is going to answer your questions or fix your problems. You are the cavalry. You are the senior leader now. How are you going to step into that role with confidence and humility? What supports or safety net do you need to build for you and your team to move forward during this time of great flux?

Go to lunch already. Part of your professional and personal safety net no doubt includes going to experts, mentors, and colleagues. Can you find time to go to coffee or lunch to meet with Boomer mentors, to update them and to see what is working well for them? I find that many of my coffees and lunches with Boomer mentors and friends are among the most uplifting and validating and leave me with not only ideas for the present but for the future as well.

Chapter Sixteen

Embracing Our Legacy as Self-Sufficient, Pragmatic Bridge Builders

At midlife, many of us feel like we are just starting to figure things out and come into our own. And yet, for those of us who have children, we see how incredibly fast time passes. One of my favorite podcasters, Gretchen Rubin (*Happier*), often notes how "the days are long and the years are short." I feel now, more than ever, that I am coming to the end of a decade of serving as a college president while watching my own son graduate from high school and head off to college. This is a time of transition for many of us, compounded by the fact that our Boomer colleagues, bosses, and mentors have retired. In the words of Mayor Victoria, she can remember starting on the Tacoma City Council as a "baby." Now she realized while in conversation that she may be the oldest council member currently serving.

While our retirement may seem many years from now, maybe we are looking daily at how we too can retire along with the Boomers. Maybe we're considering a substantive career change as we begin to embrace the empty nest. I, too, have spent time thinking about when I conclude my current career and transition to the next professional and personal chapters in my life. How do I want to leave my organization? How much of the college can I wrap into a big red bow to hand off to the next leader?

As we ask ourselves, *What's next?* can we also contemplate a little more planfully, perhaps holistically, how we want to transition into our next chapter of life and how we want to exit in a way that sets up Millennials and Gen Z for future success? Our second half of life indeed depends upon a healthy and vital Millennial and Gen Z workforce. We have some work to do in the meantime.

As we build our bridge to the future and set our younger colleagues up for success, all while maintaining rapport with our Gen X and Boomer friends and former colleagues, I suspect our legacy may not be celebrated or shouted from the rooftops. Our generational cohort may be too small. That is just fine by me. We know the work we do every day. We know our behind-the-scenes efforts to continue the Boomers high work ethic, institutional memory, and standards while pragmatically guiding and supporting younger colleagues to future success. We are uniquely positioned to do so because have always been in the shadow of the Boomers and in between the Millennials.

We know how to work across ages and stages because we have never had the experience of being surrounded by those who are only our age (except perhaps at school and college, for those who had the traditional experience). Since high school or college, we have been a key component of the work-force, too small in numbers to warrant national headlines, but large enough to play critical roles in our organizations. Our pragmatic generational zeitgeist of not being large enough for the country to bend to our whims just may be what saves us today.

GEN X LEADERSHIP REFLECTION QUESTIONS

1. Did you blaze a teleworking path in your own work? How did you do so? Was it difficult? How can you make that process seamless for your employees now?
2. Do you consider self-care part of your job? If not, why not? How can you double down at midlife?
3. How are you nurturing your network? Are you proactively expanding your network with the lens of your own longevity?
4. Are you getting the support you need to prepare for the empty nest, parental care, and retirement? Are there mental health, financial, and/ or legal advising resources that you can access if you are not doing so already?
5. Do you know how you learn best? Are you an audio, visual, and/or hands-on learner? Can you leverage how you learn best to push against the midlife leadership grind and stay curious?
6. How are you planning to learn more about the generations and, in gen-eral, push against the meme-fueled biases that we are all faced with?

ACTION STEPS: EMBRACE OUR
ROLE AS BRIDGE BUILDERS

Step into our role as senior leaders and keepers of institutional memory.
Look around. You are it. You are your own cavalry, and you now have the

necessary experience. Even if you don't feel like a senior leader and may be working through imposter syndrome, you are the leader that others look to for advice for what's next. Especially after the past few years, you can be confident that you can step into the challenges and opportunities ahead. You can handle what comes your way. You've got this, and no one else has the answer. You may not have *the* answer, but you certainly know how to get it and create solutions.

Prepare to wrap up your work in a bow and hand it off, even if you are not going anywhere. How do you want to wrap up your work as a leader where you are today? Is there a list of things you still want to accomplish? Can you create your own red bow list? So that when the time comes, you are ready to leave your organization in a better place than you found it?

Learn from Boomers *now* about what retirement really is. Now is a great time to once again learn from those Boomers who are paving the way into retirement. Are there Boomers who are creating their own businesses, cultivating interesting hobbies, or traveling to amazing places? Perhaps they are reinventing part-time work, full-time work, coaching, or consulting. Are there other lessons we can learn from them as they blaze a trail into retirement, such as the importance of good health and health care in retirement?

Put a plan together to set yourself up successfully for your 100-year life. I, too, am working on including and welcoming younger friends and family into my life. My very wise Boomer friend told me that her mother always encouraged her to have many friends at many different ages and stages in her home. Very wise counsel.

Source: Getty Images, XiaoYun Li

Conclusion

I find it ironic that I am wrapping up this book exactly a year after I began in earnest, at another presidents' summer retreat. This year, however, the exodus of Boomer colleagues did not feel as ominous. The positive energy of our new president colleagues was noted—even among my most jaded of Gen X colleagues. We held a half-day orientation for the new presidents (which was helpful for me as well). There was a sense of optimism in the room.

Most of the new presidents were Gen Xers. They provided a breath of fresh air for us all. They understood the many challenges ahead of them, yet they were genuinely happy to be at the leadership table. And most of the new presidents are Gen Xers with over twenty years of experience coming into their roles. They were very talented and competent vice-presidents, one of whom was my own highly capable vice-president, and another was a mentee. On that note, I want to underscore that there is nothing more gratifying than playing a small role in a close colleague's success and seeing one of your employees and mentees rise and thrive professionally.

Coming into this retreat, I had to laugh that the *New York Times* ran an article finally acknowledging Gen X leadership and our critical role. The title is "Gen X Is in Charge. Don't Make a Big Deal about It."[1] There is nothing like a *New York Times* headline to validate one's work.

I've included a final summary of the six action steps recommended in this book, which are intended to see you through this critical time with validation, optimism, and pragmatism. We'll get there, and while we may not get the credit, we can all rest in the satisfaction of a job well done. Like a gold star from our youth. That's really all we have ever needed or asked for—recognition of our work and the contributions that we have made, even if we still break out a flannel shirt and listen to the music of our youth occasionally (by the way, did you know the '90s are back?)

I want to wrap up this book with a proverbial big red bow of gratitude and reverence for where you are in midlife. This is a period of incredible personal and professional transition and transformation, all while being the adult everyone looks to at home and at work to get the job done. I cannot convey enough gratitude and admiration for our Leaders who were willing to share their stories of leadership, growth, and resilience.

You are *the* leader we need right now. Your lived and professional experiences, grounded in the generational zeitgeist of pragmatism and humility, are exactly what we need now. Problem solvers who are not leading with ego but instead a drive to, at some point, hand off our good work to our Millennials and Gen Z colleagues with the satisfaction that we did the best we could and moved our organizations forward, leaving them in better places than how we found them (or least inherited them post-pandemic). I wish you many more years of good health as you continue to lead us through to the multigenerational future we all want.

ACTION SUMMARY: SIX STEPS TO SUSTAIN OURSELVES AND OUR ORGANIZATIONS WHILE LEADING THROUGH THE HOT MIDDLE OF THE PANINI PRESS OF LIFE

One: Create the Organizations We Wanted at the Beginning of Our Careers

- Reflect on the organization you wanted to work at earlier in your career.
- Ask your employees what they need support with now.
- How can you continue to develop as a leader in spaces where you are not an expert?

Two: Nurture a Community of Gen X leaders

- Expand your network as wide as you can.
- Form your mastermind group.
- Find fellow empathetic leaders.
- Consider this network a critical component of your personal and professional longevity and sustainability.
- Prepare yourself for the role of adult caregiving.

Three: Stay Curious and Not Let the Grind Grind Us Down

- "It's a new day every day."
- Take care of yourself (as well as you would treat your employees).
- Ageism is real.
- Foster endless curiosity.

Four: Build the Bench While Calling the Shots

- Let go of outdated Millennial stereotypes (Millennials are forty now).
- Prepare Millennials for leadership roles when we retire.
- Center Millennials as partners, colleagues, leaders, future leaders, and friends (they need us, and we need them).

Five: Call on Gen Z to Join Us and Be the Future We Need

- Consider management-by-coaching approach for Gen Z.
- Reconsider mental health in the workforce.
- Remember, Gen Z is our future.

Six: Call in Our Boomer Retirees for Coaching, Mentoring, and Support

- Create emeritus, consulting, and part-time opportunities for Boomer mentors.
- Rebuild your safety net.
- Go to lunch already.

Embrace Our Legacy as Self-Sufficient, Pragmatic Bridge Builders

- Step into our role as senior leaders and keepers of institutional memory.
- Prepare to wrap up your work in a bow and hand it off—even if you are not going anywhere.
- Learn from Boomers about what retirement really is now.
- Put a plan together to set yourself up successfully for your 100-year life.

Source: Getty Images, XiaoYun Li

Notes

CHAPTER ONE

1. Bump, P. (2023). *Aftermath: The Last Days of the Baby Boom and the Future of Power in America*. Viking.

2. Dhawan, E. (2021, April 21). *Why the Hybrid Workforce of the Future Depends on the 'Geriatric Millennial.'* Millennials born between 1980–85 know how to work across generational divide. https://index.medium.com/why-the-hybrid-workforce-of-the-future-depends-on-the-geriatric-millennial-6f9ff4de1d23.

CHAPTER TWO

1. Powell, J. H. (2022, November 30). *Inflation and the Labor Market*. At the Hutchins Center on Fiscal and Monetary Policy, Brookings Institution, Washington, DC: https://www.federalreserve.gov/newsevents/speech/powell20221130a.htm.

2. Pham, J. (2021). *Passing on the Entrepreneurial Spirit*. https://www.linkedin.com/pulse/passing-entrepreneurial-spirit-lessons-from-my-father-julie-pham-phd. To read the original, visit: https://drjuliepham.substack.com/p/passing-on-the-entrepreneurial-spirit.; Pham, J. (2021, April). *Passing on the Entrepreneurial Spirit. Northwest Vietnamese News*. https://nvnorthwest.com/2021/04/remembering-kim-pham-nvtb-publisher-and-my-father/ (English) and https://nvnorthwest.com/2021/04/nhung-ky-niem-sau-cung-de-nho-ve-bo-than-yeu/ (Vietnamese).

3. Thornton, C. (2023, April 26). *Hate crimes will spike around the 2024 presidential election, civil rights group warns*. USA Today. https://www.usatoday.com/story/news/nation/2023/04/26/election-2024-hate-crimes-spike-anticipated/11706654002/.

4. Wheatley, M. (2017). *Who Do We Choose to Be: Facing Reality, Claiming Leadership, Restoring Sanity*. Berrett-Koehler Publishers.

CHAPTER THREE

1. Thomas, M. (1972). *Free to be you and me.* https://www.songlyrics.com/marlo-thomas/free-to-be-you-and-me-lyrics.

2. Twenge, J. (2023). *Generations: The real differences between GenZ, Millennials, GenX, Boomers, and Silents-and What they Mean for America's Future.* Atria Books.

3. Calhoun, A. (2021). *Why We Can't Sleep: Women's New Midlife Crisis.* Grove Press UK.

4. Schulte, Brigid. (2014). *Overwhelmed: Work, Love, and Play When No One Has the Time.* Sarah Crichton Books.

5. Mauseth, K. (2021, March 11). *Burnout, Compassion Fatigue, Moral Injury and Resilience in the Context of COVID-19.* [Video]. YouTube. Northwest MHTTC. https://www.youtube.com/watch?v=mep3xxOW6co.

CHAPTER FOUR

1. Tervalon, M., and Murray-García, J. (1998). "Cultural humility vs. cultural competence: A critical distinction in defining physician training outcomes in multicultural education." *Journal of Health Care for the Poor and Underserved, 9*(2), 117.

CHAPTER FIVE

1. Heuston, A. (2022). *Lead Like a Woman: Tales from the Trenches.* Prominence Publishing; Heuston, A. (2023). *Lead Like a Woman: Audacity.* Prominence Publishing; Heuston, A. (2021). *Stronger on the Other Side.* Lead Like a Woman Publishing.

2. William Serrata's EPCC bio: https://www.epcc.edu/Administration/President/biography.

3. Dr. Julie Pham's bio: https://curiositybased.com/about-us/#meetTeam.

4. Pham, J. (2022). *7 Forms of Respect.* B. C. Allen Publishing.

5. Victoria Woodard's bio: https://www.cityoftacoma.org/cms/one.aspx?pageId=10289.

CHAPTER EIGHT

1. Lee, S. (2021). *Be Water, My Friend: The Teachings of Bruce Lee.* Flatiron Books.

2. Pham, J. (2021, April). *Passing on the Entrepreneurial Spirit.* Northwest Vietnamese News. https://nvnorthwest.com/2021/04/remembering-kim-pham-nvtb-publisher-and-my-father/ (English) and https://nvnorthwest.com/2021/04/nhung-ky-niem-sau-cung-de-nho-ve-bo-than-yeu/ (Vietnamese).

CHAPTER NINE

1. Wheatley, M. (2017). *Who Do We Choose to Be: Facing Reality, Claiming Leadership, Restoring Sanity*. Berrett-Koehler Publishers.

2. Gallman, S. (2015, September 26). *Seattle college releases IDs of those killed in bus, duck boat crash*. CNN.

3. Gluckman, N. (2020, April 4). *Campus Zero: Before the coronavirus shuttered universities nationwide, it turned Seattle's college leaders into early responders. Their decisions shaped a nation's reaction.* The Chronicle of Higher Education.

4. Davis Kho, N. (2019). *The Thank-you Project*. Running Press Adult.

CHAPTER TEN

1. Learn more in order to do better, as inspired by the late Dr. Maya Angelou.

2. Angelou, M. (1978). *And Still I Rise: A Book of Poems*. Random House.

3. Rubin, G. and Craft, L. (Co-Hosts). (2015–present). *Happier with Gretchen Rubin*. Cadence 13. https://gretchenrubin.com/.

CHAPTER ELEVEN

1. DeWitte, M. (2023). *50 years on, Mark Granovetter's 'The Strength of Weak Ties' is stronger than ever.* http://news.stanford.edu/.

2. Soaring rates of new entrepreneurial efforts and businesses launched by those in midlife.

3. Twenge, J. (2023). *Generations: The Real Differences between Gen Z, Millennials, Gen X, Boomers, and Silents-and What They Mean for America's Future*. Atria Books.

4. Lee, J. (Author). (2023, April 30) The Agony of Putting Your Life on Hold to Care for Your Parents [Audio podcast episode]. *The Daily: The Sunday Read*. New York Times. https://www.nytimes.com/2023/04/30/podcasts/the-daily/sandwich-generation-parents-caring.html?searchResultPosition=13.

5. Rogers, K. (2023, June 19). *Loneliness or social isolation linked to serious health outcomes, study finds*. CNN.

6. Gratton, L. (2016). *The 100-Year Life*. Bloomsbury Information.

7. Vanderkam, L. (2022). *Tranquility by Tuesday*. Portfolio.

8. Lee, J. (Author). (2023, April 30) The Agony of Putting Your Life on Hold to Care for Your Parents [Audio podcast episode]. *The Daily: The Sunday Read*. New York Times. https://www.nytimes.com/2023/04/30/podcasts/the-daily/sandwich-generation-parents-caring.html?searchResultPosition=13.

CHAPTER TWELVE

1. Rath, T., & Gallup (2017). *StrengthsFinder 2.0.* Gallup Press.
2. Vanderkam, L. (2022) *Tranquility by Tuesday*. Portfolio.
3. Koh, C. (Host) (2023, July 6). Cultivating Hobbies and Interests. *Edit Your Life*. Adalyst Media. https://edityourlifeshow.com/cultivating-hobbies/.

CHAPTER THIRTEEN

1. Pham, J. (2022). *7 Forms of Respect*. CuriosityBased Seattle WA, B.C. Allen Publishing and Tonic Books.
2. Lee, J. (Author). (2023, April 30) The Agony of Putting Your Life on Hold to Care for Your Parents [Audio podcast episode]. *The Daily: The Sunday Read*. New York Times. https://www.nytimes.com/2023/04/30/podcasts/the-daily/sandwich -generation-parents-caring.html?searchResultPosition=13.

CHAPTER FOURTEEN

1. Twenge, J (2023). *Generations: The Real Differences between Gen Z, Millennials, GenX, Boomers and Silents—and What They Mean for America's Future*. Atria Books.
2. Slavitt, A. (Host) (2023, June 14). One Congressman's Battle With Debilitating Anxiety (with Rep. Adam Smith) [Audio Podcase Episode]. *In the Bubble*. Lemonada. https://lemonadamedia.com/podcast/in-the-bubble-one-congressmans-battle -with-debilitating-anxiety-with-rep-adam-smith/.

CHAPTER FIFTEEN

1. Dhawan, E. (2021, April 21). "Why the Hybrid Workforce of the Future Depends on the 'Geriatric Millennial' Millennials Born between 1980–85 Know How to Work across Generational Divide." Published in Index, Medium.com.

CONCLUSION

1. Goldberg, E. (2023, July 9). "Gen X Is in Charge. Don't Make a Big Deal about It." *New York Times*. https://www.nytimes.com/2023/07/07/business/gen-x-in-charge -companies-chief-executives.html.

About the Author

Amy Morrison, EdD, is a proud Gen X leader, working mother, and first-generation college graduate. She is a dedicated advocate for public workforce education with over twenty-five years of service.

Morrison has led her college, LWTech, for over a decade. Her college was the first in the country directly impacted by COVID-19.

Morrison has been recognized for her leadership with the University of Nebraska Lincoln 2020 Impact Award and as the Pacific NW 2017 Pacesetter of the Year by NCMPR.

Morrison lives near Seattle, Washington, with her multigenerational family.